JOKES
FOR ALL
OCCASIONS

AL SCHOCK

Published by
Melvin Powers
WILSHIRE BOOK COMPANY
12015 Sherman Road
No. Hollywood, California 91605
Telephone: (213) 875-1711 / (818) 983-1105

Printed by

HAL LEIGHTON PRINTING COMPANY
P.O. Box 3952
North Hollywood, California 91605
Telephone: (213) 983-1105

Library of Congress Catalog Card No.: 79-65290

Printed in the United States of America
ISBN-0-87980-368-1

JOYS THAT ARE SHARED
ARE DOUBLED

TRAGEDIES THAT ARE SHARED
ARE HALVED

TABLE OF CONTENTS

ACKNOWLEDGMENTS

To all the members of my family, my wife Phyllis, sons Bernie, Paul and Steve, and daughters Bobbi and Barb, for their willingness to serve as guinea pigs and test targets for the material contained herein, and especially for their understanding and tolerance.

To Darleen Gage for her searching and re-searching, her typing and retyping, and her patience and impatience in the preparation of this manuscript.

To the thousands of people who have heard me tell many of the stories within these covers, and a special thanks to the hundreds of emcees and speakers, many now forgotten, who directly or indirectly were the contributors of much of the material in this book.

**A GOOD LEADER
IS A PERSON
WHO SOLVES
MORE PROBLEMS
THAN HE
CREATES**

PREFACE

Knowledge, whether obtained through education or experience, coupled with productive and satisfying work, is basic to success.

But success in itself does not necessarily bring happiness. Happiness comes from being involved and by learning to share and appreciate one another. Edgar Guest, the common people's poet, wrote:

> The joy of life is living it, or so it seems
>   to me;
> In finding shackles on your wrists, then
>   struggling till you're free;
> In seeing wrongs and righting them, in
>   dreaming splendid dreams,
> Then toiling till the vision is as real as
>   moving streams.

In over a quarter of a century, as co-founder and president of my own company, I have interviewed and hired over a thousand plant and sales personnel. Though always looking for ability, aptitude and the basic skills required to do a certain job, I soon discovered that if we hired people who also possessed a good sense of humor, we assured ourselves of the acquisition of superior employees.

Though it would be wrong to generalize, I've discovered that the intelligent person who is basically devoid of a sense of humor is often not as productive as an employee who knows how and when to laugh. The ability to tell a story or use a pun can serve as a tonic or as a break in the monotony that exists to some extent in our daily lives.

This book is dedicated to all of us who seek to bring an extra measure of sunlight into our own lives and into the lives of those around us.

Al Schock

**If he can remember so many stories
And all the details that mold them
Why can't he recall with equal skill
How many times he's told them?**
—**Lucille Mannes**

INTRODUCTION

I have never taken a Dale Carnegie Course, nor have I belonged to Toastmasters. I was always afraid to. In spite of this, I've been called upon to emcee or speak at more than 2,000 functions during the past decade alone, and continue to receive over a hundred invitations annually.

Sometimes I've not been very proud of my performance, and undoubtedly would have benefited greatly from taking a specialized course in emceeing and speaking. But experience is the greatest teacher of all, and having learned from my mistakes, I have written a book on **EMCEEING (AND UNRELATED ITEMS).** The book covers everything from being yourself to overcoming nervousness, meeting hall requirements, food service, cocktail hour (or less), the use of ethnic and off-color stories, toasts, use of poetry, and many other items.

This book is an enlargement of one of the chapters in that book, namely the chapter on the use of puns, one-liners, short stories and anecdotes. I felt it would be desirable to make this material available in a single small volume.

Appropriately selected, well-told puns and stories can transform an ordinary emceeing or speaking performance into a superior one.

It would take several volumes to list the hundreds of stories and quips that I have collected, written, or embellished during my lifetime. The ones listed in this chapter have been carefully selected and most of them should be usable with some adaptation for 'a long period of time.

There are few events that cannot benefit by the interjection of a bit of frivolity or a light touch of humor. Humor, like music, is almost universally appreciated. But, as in all things, when used by emcees, moderators, speakers, whomever, good judgment and common sense must be used.

Most people with some training can tell stories and use humor with good effect for almost any occasion. When performing the function of emcee, moderator or chairperson, it is important to remember that your main function is to keep things moving and to delight the audience, when the occasion calls for it, with your own wit and humor, spiced with puns and stories that you have specifically selected for the occasion.

THE A B C's OF TELLING AND REMEMBERING STORIES

The following list will serve as a guideline for things you should remember when using puns and telling anecdotes and stories:

A. Select material suitable for the occasion.

B. Memorize it thoroughly.

C. Avoid telling the audience, "And that reminds me ..."

D. Never interrupt yourself while telling a story by saying, "Please stop me if you've heard this one before." Make the assumption, even when telling an old story, that this is the first time the audience has ever heard it. There are many old quips, anecdotes and stories that can be told in your own style and enjoyed by your audience, just as old songs are often resung and enjoyed, for instance, "My Wild Irish Rose" and "Let Me Call You Sweetheart."

E. If you find it necessary to use someone in the audience as a target for your quip or story, select that person carefully. Unless you know the person, and the story fits and has some degree of validity, using the wrong person will make you appear amateurish and your pun highly artificial. A much better practice is to use yourself in the style of a Jack Benny or a Bob Hope—"You wouldn't believe what happened to me on the way here tonight . . .", or "A funny thing happened on the way to my office this morning."

F. Make certain that the anecdotes and stories that you select fit in and are relevant, smoothly connecting even disconnected parts of your presentation as you shift gears.

G. Avoid using stories that are too involved and too long.

H. Never forget the punch line.

I. Avoid the off-color or otherwise offensive story.

J. Use associations to help you remember puns, short stories and anecdotes. Notice that in the table of contents I have used major headings to provide name associations to help you retain and recall a vast number of stories and other appropriate material. In addition to using major headings, I also suggest that you make other associations for the stories and material that you want to remember on a more or less permanent basis.

For example, let us use the first story given in this book under the heading of "Advice." The story is attributed to Frank Lloyd Wright, the famous architect. Though listing the story under "Advice" I could have also classified it under architects or builders. Few of us have a photographic mind or otherwise possess the innate intelligence to remember all things, but we can use a tool that is employed by many who practice the art of remembering things. The latter group informs us that the more absurd the association we make with the thing we want to remember, the better our chances of remembering it.

In the case of the story I've mentioned, I have made the association of this story under the major heading of "Advice", but I've also imbedded it in my mind by making the rather absurd association with Frank Lloyd Wright, the designer of the Tokyo Imperial Hotel, sitting in the lobby with water flowing through it. Now if I were asked to make comments before an architects' or builders' convention, or to make any reference concerning hotels, my mind would immediately recall for me the Frank Lloyd Wright story.

Let's take another example. Go to the section in the book under the major heading of "Agriculture." The first story listed under this heading pertains to the Texas rancher who came to South Dakota to visit his farmer friend. In connection with my work I have spoken to many farm groups and organizations. This particular story when told is always well received by a rural audience. To be sure that I would always remember it, I have associated this particular story with a big Texan sitting at the wheel of a small dilapidated 1930 Model T Ford, and a rather smallish farmer sitting at his side. Having made this association, I have no difficulty in recalling the story for possible use whenever I address a group of agriculturalists, Texans, or even an automotive group.

The point to be made in the above two

illustrations is that in order to remember things, unless you are especially gifted, you must make associations that enhance your recall abilities. The associations made under the major headings in this book or others that you might devise will be most helpful. Additionally, to imbed in your mind the things you really want to remember, make associations that are somewhat out of the ordinary—indeed absurd. If you do this you will soon surprise yourself with the great amount of material that you will readily recall which will be usable for you on many needed occasions.

ADVICE

Frank Lloyd Wright, the famous architect, had designed a home for a client. Shortly after the home had been built, the client called Mr. Wright and said, "Mr. Wright, you know that home that you built for me? The roof is leaking and the basement is full of water. What shall I do?"

To which Mr. Wright replied, "Try to rise above it."

A lady had a problem with a skunk in her cellar. She called the local conservation officer. He said, "All you have to do is to spread a trail of bread crumbs from the basement on out and the skunk will follow it."

Two days later the lady called back and said, "I did what you told me, but now I have two skunks in my basement."

Make someone happy today—resign.

Lord, Lord, use me in Thy work—especially in an advisory capacity.

AGRICULTURE

A Texas rancher, visiting a South Dakota farmer friend, asked him to show him his farm. After seeing the 1,000 acre spread, the Texan bragged that down home he could get into his car, drive all day, and by evening would not have gotten to the distant point of his ranch.

The South Dakotan simply replied, "You know, I had a car like that once."

☆ ☆ ☆

A farmer went to see the veterinary about his sick horse. After describing the symptoms, the veterinarian said, "Here are some pills to give to the horse."

"How on earth," inquired the farmer, "will I get the horse to take these pills?"

"Well, here's a long tube. You put the pills in the tube, you put the tube in the horse's mouth, and then you blow."

A couple of days later, the veterinarian asked the farmer how his horse was doing.

"Well, the horse is okay, but I'm not feeling so well."

"Why?" inquired the veterinarian.

Whereupon the farmer responded, "Well, sir, the horse blew first."

☆ ☆ ☆

A farmer is a man outstanding in his field.

☆ ☆ ☆

My dad was no Burbank, but he was the first man to cross an Idaho potato with a sponge. It wasn't an especially good eating potato, but it sure held a lot of gravy.

The price of hogs had plummeted. Two farmers were discussing the situation. Said one, "If the price of hogs doesn't go up pretty soon, I'm going to have to rob a bank to make ends meet."
Whereupon his heavily mortgaged farmer friend replied, "I think I already have."

Pray for rain, but keep on hoeing.

The farmer is the first person to learn that there is no such thing as a free lunch.

There once was a red potato and a white potato. They grew up and got married and had a little sweet potato, who when she grew up wanted to marry Jack Anderson, but her parents wouldn't allow it b e c a u s e he was a commentator.

Farmers are
A hopeful set;
The more they farm
The less they net.

☆ ☆ ☆

Brigham Young said never steal a horse, for it costs more to hide it than it's worth.

A city man went out to visit his farmer friend. When he arrived at the farm, the farmer was hitching up his mule. The city man patted the mule on the back, and when he came to, the farmer said, "Your intentions were good, but your approach was wrong."

You can teach a horse how to drool, but you can't make him spit.

A tourist traveling through South Dakota noticed the large number of cattle out in the pastures. He stopped and asked a native son, "How do you account for so many cattle in your state?"
"We prefer 'em," he replied.

A county agent is a person who knows enough to tell others how to farm, but is too smart to try it himself.

☆ ☆ ☆

It was so dry that you were able to brand two calves at a time using carbon paper.

☆ ☆ ☆

It was so dry that even Baptists had to resort to sprinkling.

☆ ☆ ☆

If you cross a rooster with a rooster, you come up with a really cross rooster.

There's an old Chinese saying: "Give a man a fish and you feed him for a day. Teach him how to fish and you feed him for a lifetime."

A rancher asked a veterinarian for some free advice. "I have a horse," he said, "that walks normally sometimes, and sometimes he·limps. What shall I do?"
The veterinarian replied, "The next time he walks normally, sell him."

Most farmers would rather haul more money to the bank than grain to the elevator.

The city politician was on his way to woo voters in ranching country. His local host was trying to fill him in on the issues which were important to the voters in the area. "Whatever you do, speak in favor of open range," he said. "These ranchers are very touchy about that."
The politician agreed to support the open range policy, and opened his speech by stating, "I understand you fellows like the open range policy. I agree with you and will fight to keep it the way you want it. But first, I'm going to do something about getting all those gosh-darned cows off the road."

11

AUTOMOTIVE

If you drive carelessly, your car will last you a lifetime.

☆　☆　☆

"And how did you manage to run over that little sports car?"
"Well sir, I looked right and I looked left, but I plumb forgot to look down."

☆　☆　☆

"Aren't you the fellow that sold me this car two weeks ago?"
"Yes, sir," said the salesman proudly.
"Well, then, tell me about it again. I get so discouraged."

☆　☆　☆

The man who pokes fun at his wife for not being able to drive the car into the garage usually sobers up when he tries to thread a needle.

☆　☆　☆

The other day I did what I've wanted to do ever since 1950—I bought myself a 1950 Cadillac!

☆　☆　☆

My wife (husband) doesn't drive the car—she (he) aims it.

☆　☆　☆

Our youngster parks cars by sound.

　　☆　☆　☆

For that rundown feeling, try jaywalking.

Our new car seats only two, but it can accommodate ten bumper stickers.

Why in the world is it always the third car back that is the first to see the light turn green?

A motorist seeing a small sports car overturned on the side of the road brought his car to a screeching halt and then rushed over to ask the young man standing beside the overturned car, "Anybody hurt?"
The young man replied, "Heck, no. I'm just changing a tire."

The service station attendant filling the tank of a big gas burner asked the motorist, "Do you mind shutting it off for a minute or two? It's getting ahead of me."

"If you let me drive, I'll be an angel," she said. He did and she was.

"Didn't you see that red light?" the cop asked.
"Sure, but when you've seen one red light, you've seen them all."

AWARDS

My friend got the poultry award of the year for egg production by putting up a picture of Colonel Sanders in his chicken house.

Two out of each three Americans get at least one award annually. The rest take their trading stamps down to the redemption center.

BACHELOR

A bachelor is a man who goes to a drive-in movie on a motorcycle.

☆　☆　☆

A bachelor is a man with an un-altar-able view.

☆　☆　☆

A bachelor is a man that comes to work from a different direction every morning.

☆　☆　☆

A bachelor is a man who has not made the same mistake once.

☆　☆　☆

A bachelor is a man who does not believe in feathering his own nest.

☆　☆　☆

BALDNESS AND BARBERS

One thing you can say for baldness is that it is neat.

☆ ☆ ☆

Some have to come out on top to set shining examples.

☆ ☆ ☆

Old barbers never die, they just can't cut it like they used to.

☆ ☆ ☆

If you're losing a little on the top, cheer up. You're probably gaining it back in the middle.

☆ ☆ ☆

The young are getting taller, the tops of their heads keep pushing through their hair.

☆ ☆ ☆

Just because there is no snow on the roof does not mean that there is no fire in the furnace.

☆ ☆ ☆

Research shows that baldness at the back of the head indicates a thinker; baldness at the front of the head a lover; and a man who is bald all over just thinks he's a lover.

☆ ☆ ☆

Looking at my bald head makes me think of heaven—there is no parting there.

☆ ☆ ☆

When the Lord makes something good, He doesn't cover it up.

☆ ☆ ☆

People with good growth on their heads don't necessarily have well-fertilized minds.

☆ ☆ ☆

A sign of wealth is when a bald man gets a haircut.

☆ ☆ ☆

BANKING

A native American Indian went to see his banker about a loan. "Do you have any collateral?" the banker inquired.

The Indian said he had no idea what collateral was.

"Well, do you have any property?"

"No," said the Indian, "only twenty horses."

"That'll be fine," the banker said and took the horses as collateral.

A couple of months later the borrower returned with a $5,000 check, and as he cashed it to pay off his original $500 loan, the banker said, "We'll be happy to keep the balance on deposit for you."

And the Indian replied, "How many horses do you have?"

☆ ☆ ☆

A Texan wrote a check on our bank and the bank bounced.

☆ ☆ ☆

Their joint account's retarded
By one persistent flaw.
He's fast on the deposit,
But she's quicker on the draw.
    —Author Unknown

☆ ☆ ☆

BIRTHDAY

Often you can surprise your spouse on his or her birthday just by mentioning it.

☆ ☆ ☆

On her birthday, he gave his wife a plot in the cemetery.
The following year he gave her nothing.
"Why no present this year?" she inquired.
"Well," he replied, "you haven't used the one I gave you last year."

☆ ☆ ☆

I'm only twenty nine, but it's my second time around.

☆ ☆ ☆

I'm plenty-nine and holding.

☆ ☆ ☆

BORN LOSER

The window washer who steps back to admire his own work.

☆ ☆ ☆

The business man who starts a hog farm in Israel.

☆ ☆ ☆

The person who absent-mindedly raises the thermostat in his own wax museum.

☆ ☆ ☆

The hitchhiker who was sucking his thumb when a car went by.

☆ ☆ ☆

BOSS

I'm just like the rest of you around here—just a number. The only difference is that I'm number one.

To the secretary, "This is the earliest you've ever been late."

In my house I'm the boss. I wear the pants, even though they're protected with an apron.

A good boss is a person who takes a little more than his share of the blame and a little less than his share of the credit.

A boss who gets to work at 8 a.m. and opens all his own mail must have something to conceal.

☆ ☆ ☆

BUSINESS

Every business has its problems but there is no problem like no business.

☆   ☆   ☆

A customer came into the supermarket near closing. She asked the butcher for a nice chicken. He brought one out and put it on the scale and said it weighed three and a half pounds.

She wanted a larger one, so he stepped back into the cooler and discovered that there were no more. So he brought it back out and said, "Ma'am, I've got one here that's almost four pounds."

"That will do," she said. "I'll take them both."

☆   ☆   ☆

A recession is a period when you tighten your belt. A depression is a time when you have no belt to tighten. And when you have no trousers to hold up, man, that's a panic.

☆   ☆   ☆

The big corporations have no monopoly. Their problems are so broad and diverse that they have little time for details. Small business-men who tackle the tiny things that are overlooked by big corporations can make a killing. Thousands have done it and thousands more will do it.

☆   ☆   ☆

The counselor asked the employee how long he had been working at the company. He said, "Ever since they tried to fire me."

☆　☆　☆

How to succeed in business without really trying?
Embezzle company funds.

☆　☆　☆

A merchant was having his sales clerk stock some shelves. The clerk noticed that the invoice cost was $1 per unit and he was asked to put a sales price of $4 on each item. "Boss," he said, "isn't that taking too much of a mark-up?"
"What's wrong with three per cent?" fired back his employer.

☆　☆　☆

The young executive came home and told his wife that he had just been made vice president at the bank. She said, "Oh, that's nothing. They have so many vice presidents now that down at the grocery store where I shop they even have a vice president in charge of the prune department."
He didn't believe her, so she said, "Why don't you call our grocery store?"
So he called and asked the person that answered, "Will you please give me the vice president of the prune department?"
Back came the response, "Bulk or packaged?"

☆　☆　☆

The reverend was admonishing his parishioners on the evils of sin.

"Remember, my friends," he said, "there will be no buying or selling in heaven."

A disgruntled old gent in the back row shouted back, "That's not where business is going, anyway."

An executive is that type of person that solves more problems than he creates.

Our government states that it is a 50-50 partner with business. Sometimes I wish it would choose another partner.

We are expecting another baby—business is expanding on all fronts.

American business need never apologize. If the entire world population of over three and a half billion people were compressed into 1,000 people, only 60 would be Americans, representing over six per cent of the world's population. But they would possess one half of the total income, one half of the capital, and would have material possessions at least 15 times greater than the possessions of all the other 940 people in the world. And the lifespan of the Americans would be approximately twice that of all the others. A system that has achieved such miracles can't be all bad.

There's a lot of free cheese in mousetraps, but you don't find any happy mice there.

☆ ☆ ☆

How to be successful in 1976? Go to work and stay at it.

☆ ☆ ☆

To err is human, to forgive is against company policy.

☆ ☆ ☆

Who's afraid of recessions? I've failed during boom times.

☆ ☆ ☆

A desk is a wastebasket with drawers.

☆ ☆ ☆

CAPITAL PUNISHMENT

Anyone who believes in capital punishment ought to be hanged.

The man condemned to die in the electric chair asked his minister if he had any parting words of wisdom for him. Whereupon the reverend replied, "Yes, don't sit down."

As the minister was leaving the execution chamber, the condemned man implored him to please hold his hand.

The cure for crime is not the electric chair, but the high chair.

CHARISMA

He has so much charm that if he told you to go to hell, you could hardly wait to get started.

☆　☆　☆

Charm is something people have until they begin to rely upon it.

☆　☆　☆

Charm and wit and levity
May help one at the start,
But in the end it's brevity
That wins the public's heart.
—Anon

☆　☆　☆

CHILDREN

A night is something to get the children through.

☆ ☆ ☆

"Why didn't you brush your teeth?" asked the mother of her seven-year-old.
"I couldn't, Mom," he said, "the battery is dead."

☆ ☆ ☆

The Boy Scout came to his troop meeting with a black eye. When asked what had happened, he said that he had tried to help an elderly lady across the street.
"How in the world," asked the Scoutleader, "did you get a black eye doing that?"
"Well," the young Scout replied, "she didn't want to go."

☆ ☆ ☆

The Sunday School teacher told her class, "Now, children, I want you to be so quiet that you can hear a pin drop."
After a few seconds of total quiet, a little boy yelled, "Okay, teacher, let her drop."

☆ ☆ ☆

I'm the father of five children—all white. This is quite a miracle when you stop to think about it. Did you know every third child born in the world today is Chinese?

☆ ☆ ☆

Spank your children every day. If you don't know what for, they will.

If your children don't consider you an embarrassment at an early age, they don't have proper parents. (from M. S. Forbes)

I told my young boy to go to the end of the line, but he came back and said, "Dad, there's someone already there."

Little children, little trouble; big children, big trouble.

Kids don't go to camp, they are sent there.

The easiest children to bring up are calm, thoughtful, and somebody else's.

The number of perfect children in the world is directly proportional to the number of average parents.

CIVIL RIGHTS

"What do you think of the Civil Rights Bill?" asked the constituent of his congressman.

He replied, "If we owe it, I think we ought to pay it."

☆ ☆ ☆

Black is beautiful. So are understanding and tolerance.

On the first morning that busing commenced in response to a judge's order to achieve minimum standards of integration, the bus driver, at his first pickup point, stepped out of the bus and announced to the children, "This morning you are neither black nor white — you are all green. Now, those of you that are dark green will go to the rear of the bus."

☆ ☆ ☆

COMMITTEE

The unable appointed by the unwilling to do the unnecessary.

☆ ☆ ☆

The camel is a horse that was put together by a committee.

☆ ☆ ☆

God so loved the world that he did not leave it in the hands of a committee.

☆ ☆ ☆

COMMUNICATION

A gentleman desirous of obtaining a parrot that could speak two languages kept searching for several months. One day the operator of the local pet shop called him and said that he had just such a parrot. On arriving at the pet shop, the operator informed the prospective customer that the parrot spoke not two languages, but five. He was delighted. So he said, "Just send the cage and the parrot to my home. My wife will be there to receive it."

When the purchaser arrived at home at six o'clock that evening, he asked his wife, "What is for dinner?"

"You should ask," she replied. "You sent it home this afternoon."

"Do you mean to tell me, dear, that you cooked the parrot that I sent home? The one I've been searching for for such a long time? And did you know that the parrot could speak not only two languages, but five?"

"Why, then," asked his wife, "didn't he speak up?"

Advertising pays, but there is no sense in advertising our troubles. There is no market for them.

On the big island of Hawaii game officials discovered that the mongoose was a predator of the rat. An official on a neighboring island, having a rat problem, felt that he should like to import a pair of mongooses. So he wrote a letter to the game official on the big island. He started out by stating, "Dear sir, will you please send me two mongeese."

Thinking that his English was not correct, he tore it up and gave it a second try. This time he wrote, "Dear sir, will you please send me two mongeeses?" This still didn't sound quite right, so he tore it up once more and gave it a third try. This time he wrote, "Dear sir, will you please send me one mongoose. Thank you very much. Sincerely."

Then he signed it, adding this P.S.: "Aw, shucks, inasmuch as you're sending me one, why don't you throw another one into the box?"

☆ ☆ ☆

COMPLIMENTS

Though the distance between the two is only 11 inches, the results received from a pat on the back or a kick in the pants are vastly different.

You get most credit by giving credit to those whom credit is due.

Flattery will not hurt you so long as you don't inhale it.

DAIRY

Times were tough and the farmer was having a difficult time. He was so tired that even the cow he was milking became a wee bit irked. And the cow said, "If you can just hang on a little bit longer, I'll jump up and down."

☆ ☆ ☆

If you want to cry over spilled milk, condense it.

☆ ☆ ☆

I have a farm background—a family of 10, milked 42 cows, no problem—we all pulled together.

☆ ☆ ☆

For two decades there has been considerable talk about the high cholesterol content of foods. In the mid-50's, Dr. Ancel Keyes was a great proponent of low cholesterol diets and implicated dairy products as being high in cholesterol content. Following is one dairyman's reply:
"We all have to go, Dr. Keyes,
But the guy with the heart goes with ease,
So why give up butter and cheese
And wait for some ghastly disease?"

☆ ☆ ☆

Milk is the only liquid that has enough sense to sour naturally.

☆ ☆ ☆

A cow is the quadruped titular head of the bovine family.

☆ ☆ ☆

Why is it that Swiss cheese has all the holes when it's limburger that needs the ventilation?

☆ ☆ ☆

Two cows in a pasture near a highway saw a tank truck pass by with a sign on the side reading, "Pasteurized, homogenized, standardized, and vitamin D added."
One turned to the other and remarked, "Makes you feel sort of inadequate, doesn't it?"

☆ ☆ ☆

"How do you put those holes into Swiss cheese?"
"It's easy, we just use whole milk."

☆ ☆ ☆

That's udderly ridiculous.

☆ ☆ ☆

I should like to hear the udder side.

☆ ☆ ☆

You know what we dairymen think of substitutes.

☆ ☆ ☆

Smile when you say "cheese."

☆ ☆ ☆

Milk: The udder cola.

☆ ☆ ☆

You can make cheese at home, for where there's a will there's whey.

☆ ☆ ☆

A Quaker was milking his cow when she switched her tail, hitting him in the eye and causing a severe burning sensation. The cow had done this several times. He could stand it no longer, so he set down his bucket and went around the stanchion and stood directly in front of the cow, and said, "Thou knowest that I'm a Quaker. Thou also knowest that I canst smite thee. But what thou does not know is that I can sell thee to my Lutheran friend, and he can beat the holy h—— out of you."

☆ ☆ ☆

DECISIONS

Indecision is a form of hell on earth.

Learn to make decisions quickly but be careful in giving your reasons. Your decisions are often right, but your reasons are wrong.

☆   ☆   ☆

Decide and be done with it.

☆   ☆   ☆

Decide—make yourself vulnerable.

☆   ☆   ☆

DENTIST

Do you promise to pull the tooth, the whole tooth, and nothing but the tooth?

☆ ☆ ☆

Teeth are very nice to have,
They fill you with content;
If you do not know it now,
You will when they have went!

☆ ☆ ☆

"Mom, I can't brush my teeth. The battery is dead."

☆ ☆ ☆

DIETING

There is a new diet that is very effective. You only eat when there's good news.

There's a new Chinese diet out—eat all you want, but you're allowed only one chopstick.

I got on the scale and it said come back—when you're alone.

The best way to diet is to keep your mouth shut and your refrigerator closed.

My wife is on a diet where she's losing five pounds per week. I've calculated in 30 weeks I'll be completely rid of her.

There's a new diet called the sample diet—you can taste all the food you want to, but if it tastes good, you have to spit it out.

My wife is on a diet where she eats all she wants to one day and then she fasts for two days. It's called the rhythm method of girth control.

☆ ☆ ☆

My doctor has just put me on a new diet. He told me that I could eat anything that I liked, and then he gave me a list of the foods that I like.

The dieter asked the waiter, "Is this plate damp?" "No," was the reply, "that's your soup."

"How did you find your steak?"
"It was easy. I moved the potato over, and there it was."

A diet is for people who are thick and tired of it.

☆ ☆ ☆

A lady was drinking so much Metracal that she ended up winning the No-belly prize.

☆ ☆ ☆

Kate Smith said the world's most effective diet consists of four words, "No more, thank you."

☆ ☆ ☆

The hardest part of a diet is not watching what you eat—it's watching what others eat.

☆ ☆ ☆

If your back aches, your feet are large, and you overeat, then you are normal.

☆ ☆ ☆

I'm in good shape for the shape that I'm in.

A physician gave one of his women patients a batch of appetite-curbing pills to aid her weight reduction. He warned her not to take more than three a day. Later, her youngsters, ages 3 and 5, got hold of the pills and gobbled them down. The frightened mother called her physician immediately for advice. "Nothing too serious," the medico told her, "but the kids will be wide awake, perhaps nervous and full of steam for two or three days." He was right. The kids really went wild and led the mother a merry chase. Result: She lost six pounds from the wear and tear.

☆ ☆ ☆

DRINKING

"The way to become an alcoholic," said the confirmed drunkard, "is to take a drink and then you feel like a new man, and then he needs a drink."

☆ ☆ ☆

The professor was demonstrating before his class the ill effects of alcohol. He took a worm and dropped it into a beaker of water. The worm just continued to wiggle about. Then he dropped the worm into a beaker of alcohol and immediately the worm died. Then he asked the class what that proved. A young man replied, "Professor, that just proves that people that drink don't have worms."

☆ ☆ ☆

"Do you drink to excess?"
"Yes, I'll drink to anything."

☆ ☆ ☆

A drunk got lost in a cemetery on his way home. When he woke up he asked himself, "If I'm alive, why am I lying here among the tombstones? If I'm dead, why do I have to go to the bathroom?"

☆ ☆ ☆

An announcement from the emcee: "Sir, I've just been informed that your coat in the lobby is leaking."

☆ ☆ ☆

If drinking is bad for you, why are there so many old drunks and so few old doctors?

☆　☆　☆

A drunk was dragging a chain into the hotel lobby late one night. A bystander asked, "How come you're pulling around a chain?"

The drunk responded, "Did you ever try to push one?"

☆　☆　☆

"That was the best Scotch whiskey I ever drank. I killed a quart at 5 a.m. and then attended Mass."

"What's so great about that?"

"I'm Jewish."

☆　☆　☆

In our mountain country in Kentucky it is hard to eke out the bare necessities, and often they're not even fit to drink.

☆　☆　☆

The bus driver asked one of his regular passengers, "Did you get home all right last night?"

"Yeah, why?"

"Well, when you got up to give a lady your seat you were the only one on the bus."

☆　☆　☆

A drunk was walking with one foot in the gutter and one on the sidewalk.

"My," said a passerby, "you must be drunk."

"Thank God," said the drunk, "I thought I was a cripple."

☆　☆　☆

The liquor truck ran over my Scotchman friend. It was the first time that the drinks were on him.

☆ ☆ ☆

A universal joint is a tavern in outer space.

☆ ☆ ☆

I've never been drunk, just overserved.

☆ ☆ ☆

They formed a new club for drunk drivers. When you get four tickets you turn them in for a new bicycle.

☆ ☆ ☆

It's okay to drink like a fish if you drink what the fish drinks.

☆ ☆ ☆

Small fry to father: "How come soda pop will spoil my dinner and martinis give you an appetite?"

☆ ☆ ☆

EDUCATION

A doctor can bury his mistakes, an architect can cover his up, a farmer can plow his under, but a teacher's mistakes grow up and may become members of school boards.

There are doctors of philosophy, doctors of science, doctors of theology, doctors of this and that. The prefix "doctor" has about as much meaning as the curl in a pig's tail. It doesn't add anything to the value of the hog, but it sure tickles the ham.

I once had two teachers—one had no principle, and the other had no class.

☆ ☆ ☆

Life is a risk,
Nothing is sure,
Except for a professor
Who's got his tenure.

☆ ☆ ☆

"Education is a good thing, and blessed is the person who has it."
—Brigham Young

☆ ☆ ☆

ELECTRICIANS

Old electricians never die—they just get defused.

☆ ☆ ☆

Two repairmen were working on the power lines in front of the widow's home. The repair work required some soldering using hot metal. Inadvertantly, the man at the top of the pole spilled some hot solder and it hit his buddy on the back of the neck, slid down his back, and out the bottom of his pants leg. There was a profuse and immediate outburst of profanity directed by the victim against his buddy doing the repair work. The widow was shocked by it all and called the power company officials to complain about the abusive language that had been used.

The two workmen were called in to explain exactly what happened. The man doing the soldering said, "I accidentally dropped some of the hot metal. Unfortunately, it hit Jim who was standing at the bottom of the pole."

"What," asked the manager, "did you do, Jim?"

"Well," he said, "I just looked up at Bob and I said, "Bob, you must never allow that to happen again."

☆ ☆ ☆

EMCEEING

Humility is not one of my faults, but if I had one that would be it.

☆ ☆ ☆

Some bring happiness wherever they go, others whenever they go.

☆ ☆ ☆

If you have been looking for someone lousy— I'm it.

☆ ☆ ☆

I'm a self-made man. That relieves the Lord of all responsibility.

☆ ☆ ☆

The introduction was better than I expected, but worse than I deserved.

☆ ☆ ☆

Laugh a little faster. Time is short.

☆ ☆ ☆

Careful research has shown that it takes an emcee 10 minutes to introduce a man that needs no introduction.

☆ ☆ ☆

I have a photographic mind. I've just never had it developed.

☆ ☆ ☆

You may now raise your eyes and look upon me.

Responding to the introducer: "May the Lord forgive you for the perjury you have just committed. But on the other hand, I hope that all the rest of you will accept it as Holy Writ."

I trace my ancestry all the way back to the Boston Tea Party. It was my great-great Aunt Ella. She was the last bag that they threw into the ocean.

Always be sincere even if you don't mean it.

It's nice to be among friends, even if you are not mine.

☆ ☆ ☆

I feel like a fugitive from the law of averages.

☆ ☆ ☆

Women need no introduction. They can speak for themselves.

☆ ☆ ☆

I would like to say that this is the brightest audience that I have ever appeared before—but I can't.

☆ ☆ ☆

This is certainly a dense—I mean large crowd.

☆ ☆ ☆

Good evening, spouses and your spices.

As I introduce the head table, I would ask that they smile brightly, and then when we're all through, we'll have you give them thunderous applause.

After the audience applauds, you might say, "I wish I had your confidence."

You're my kind of audience—trapped!

Talk is cheap. The supply is larger than the demand.

I asked the speaker whether he was married. His reply, "Guilty."

☆ ☆ ☆

Good evening, fellow human beings.

☆ ☆ ☆

Will you please all rise and jog in place for 16 seconds?

☆ ☆ ☆

ENVIRONMENT AND ECOLOGY

The smog in Los Angeles is so bad that a friend of mine shot an arrow into the air and it stuck right there.

That stream is so turbid that there are fish in it that are three years old and still don't know how to swim.

The air is so polluted that you can cut it.

☆ ☆ ☆

Here's my report card, Dad, and it's bad again. What do you suppose is the matter with me anyway, heredity or environment?

☆ ☆ ☆

All those in favor of saving gas, raise your right foot.

☆ ☆ ☆

The most common insect found around these parts is the litterbug.

EPITAPHS

I always told them that I wasn't feeling so well.

☆ ☆ ☆

It isn't the cough
That sends you off.
It's the coffin
They send you off-in.

☆ ☆ ☆

Long after I have disappeared
In time's eternal mists
I know my name will still remain
On all the sucker lists.

      —Jane Saunders

☆ ☆ ☆

ETHNIC STORIES

NOTE TO THE READER:
Note that in some of the following ethnic stories we have left blanks so that if you wish to use this type of story you can fill in the name of the nationality most prevalent in your area.

☆　☆　☆

A _____ called up the local auto club and wanted to know if they could send a man to open his car because he had locked himself out. The man at the office stated that he was pretty busy, but that he would be out in a couple of hours. The motorist then replied, "I hope you can make it sooner, it's starting to rain and I left the top down."

☆　☆　☆

A _____ invented a new type of parachute. It opens on impact.

☆　☆　☆

Do you know why _____ don't hunt elephants any more? The decoys are too heavy.

☆　☆　☆

Do you know why _____ don't kill any flies? They are the national bird.

☆　☆　☆

I want to tell a story. Are there any _____ in the audience?
Well, in that case I'll tell it slowly.

☆　☆　☆　　　　　53

My two _____ friends drove to Minneapolis the other day. By the time they got there, they had cleaned 10 rest rooms.

☆ ☆ ☆

I'm a _____. I can't help it, I'm taking pills for it.

☆ ☆ ☆

"Do you know how to keep a _____ in suspense?"
"I'll tell you tomorrow."

☆ ☆ ☆

"My birthday is on March 31."
"What year?"
"Every year."

☆ ☆ ☆

"Answer the door."
"Hello, door."

☆ ☆ ☆

"Call me a cab."
"You're a cab."

☆ ☆ ☆

"Did you hear about the smart _____?"
"Relax, it's only a rumor."

☆ ☆ ☆

"How do _____ spell farm?"
"E-I-E-I-O."

☆ ☆ ☆

The _____ are so dumb they don't know how to make a bad product.

☆ ☆ ☆

An Italian immigrant with a distinct accent was bragging about his three children. "My first-a bambino, he's-a doctor. He's-a one of the best-a in his field. He make-a the $50,000 per year. My second bambino is a lawyer, and he make-a the $75,000 per year. My thirda boy, he's-a my finest boy. He's-a sports-a mechanic."

"What," inquired my friend, "is a 'sportsamechanic'?"

"He's-a person that fixes the football games, the basketball games, and all-a the other sportsa-games."

☆　☆　☆

Mexicans are not lazy, they just enjoy a high standard of living.

☆　☆　☆

Three men had been sentenced to death by the guillotine in France. One was a Frenchman, one was a Englishman, and one was a German. The guillotine had not been used for some time. The first man to be strapped in was the Frenchman. The screws were loosened, but because the knife had rusted into the frame, it moved just a little bit. The rules said if the knife didn't fall, the man would go free. The second person to be strapped in was the Englishman. The same thing happened, although the knife moved down a little farther in the frame. The next was the German. And just as the executioner was ready to loosen the screws, the German looked up and said, "Hey, you would have better luck with your operation if you would put a little oil in the knife-carrying frame."

☆　☆　☆

Recently I met a handsome man with a Nordic accent. I asked him whether he was Swedish or Norwegian. He said, "I'm Norwegian, but it's about the same."

☆　☆　☆

There are no paratroopers. The reason is that they can't count to ten.

☆　☆　☆

EXPERTS

A young professor had been invited to address a poultry convention. "The first thing you must do," he said, "to properly raise a flock is to separate the male chicks from the female chicks."

After he finished, a lady inquired, "Professor, how can you tell male chicks from female chicks?"

"Well," he said, "You go out into your yard and dig a pailful of worms. Then you set them before the chicks, and the male chicks will eat the male worms and the female chicks will eat the female worms."

"Yes, but, Professor, how do you tell a male worm from a female worm?"

"Madam," came the answer, "I'm a poultry expert, not a worm expert."

☆ ☆ ☆

An expert is an ordinary guy 50 miles from home.

☆ ☆ ☆

FISHING

He caught a fish so big that the negative weighed five pounds.

☆ ☆ ☆

The fish measured four inches between the eyes — via the gullet.

☆ ☆ ☆

Fisherman's prayer:
Lord, grant that I may catch a fish
So large that even I
When speaking of it afterwards
Will have no need to lie.

☆ ☆ ☆

A boy was fishing off the dock through a small hole in the ice. A larger boy came by and said, "You must be a dumb nut. If you catch a big fish, you can't bring him in."
The youth replied, "You're the dumb nut. If I catch a big fish, he can't pull me through the hole."

☆ ☆ ☆

It is impossible for Noah to have spent all his time fishing while on the Ark. Remember he had only two worms.

☆ ☆ ☆

There are two periods when fishing is good. Before you get there and after you leave.

☆ ☆ ☆

There are two kinds of fishermen—those who fish for sport and those that catch something.

☆ ☆ ☆

A fisherman who was also somewhat of an imbiber related the following story:

"I was fishing," he said, "but the fish would bite only on frogs. In searching for frogs which were rather scarce in a weed patch at the edge of the lake, I saw this big garden snake with a frog in its mouth. I tried to pull the frog out, but the snake wouldn't release him. So I took my bottle and poured some whiskey on the snake's head, and he coughed up the frog. I baited my hook with the frog, and went back to fishing. Everything was going well until I felt something crawling up my pants leg. I looked down and there was the same garden snake with another frog in his mouth."

☆ ☆ ☆

Two fishermen were discussing last year's hunting and fishing success. The topper came when one fellow said, "I and my buddy went duck hunting. A nice flock of mallards came over this pond, and would you believe that with one single shot I got my limit of five ducks. Unfortunately, they all landed out in the middle of the pond. Not having a dog, I put on my waders and went out to get them. The water was a little deep, and spilled over into my waders. When I came back to shore with my ducks and emptied out my waders, I discovered that I also had my limit of fish."

☆ ☆ ☆

FOREIGN AFFAIRS

The guy with a mane in Spain stays mostly on the plane.

☆ ☆ ☆

The seven wonders of the world
    were built with sweat and blood and stone,
But the wondrous thing about them all
Is that they were built without a U.S. loan.
Author Unknown

☆ ☆ ☆

The way to solve the Mideast problem is to get the Jews and the Israelis to live like Christians.

☆ ☆ ☆

I don't know how the Russians do it. Whenever I drink vodka, I say yes.

☆ ☆ ☆

To our Arab sheiks,
Let's not be rude;
Let's remember, they're the ones
Who send us crude.

☆ ☆ ☆

Foreignade — the refreshment that never pauses.

☆ ☆ ☆

He was tripping, not tippling, through the Orient.

☆ ☆ ☆

There is a new type of fruit drink—it's called foreign-aid. It's the pause that never refreshes.

Where's the capital of the U.S.A.? Spread all over the world.

☆　☆　☆

FRIENDS

"May I have a dime to call my friend?"
"Here's 30 cents, call all of them."

We should love our enemies, but we should also treat our friends just a wee bit better.

I have no enemies—just a few fellows on my list in case I change my mind.

I have no enemies—I've outlived most of them and I've made friends with the others.

Be kind to your friends, without them you'd be a stranger.

☆ ☆ ☆

I have friends I haven't even used yet.

☆ ☆ ☆

A friend in need is a pest.

☆ ☆ ☆

A friend who ain't in need is a friend indeed.

☆ ☆ ☆

A friend in need is a friend to avoid.

A man paraphrasing a statement attributed to Mark Twain, said that if you find a hungry dog feed him, he will not bite you and will become your best friend — and that is the main difference between man and dog.

They were friends until debt did them part.

Friends are people that have the same enemies you do.

FUND RAISING

The armed robber pointed a gun at the proprietor and said, "Give, it will make you feel better."

There are fund drives for about everything under the sun. Recently I heard about one where they were raising money for the widow of the unknown soldier.

Peter Marshall said that life is not measured so much by one's duration as by one's donation.

Loving and giving
Make life worth living.

GAMBLING

Las Vegas—now there's a town for my money.

If you go to Las Vegas to gamble, the best advice I can give any of you is that when you get off the plane, back right into the propeller, because that way you're sure to get an even split.

I was lucky in Las Vegas. I got a ride home.

And then there was the man that went to Las Vegas in a $15,000 Cadillac and came home in a $40,000 Greyhound bus.

Our three year old can count—one, two, three, four, five, six, seven, eight, nine, ten, Jack, Queen, King.

☆ ☆ ☆

They have something new in Las Vegas. It's called instant bankruptcy.

☆ ☆ ☆

Some think gambling is a sin only if you lose.

☆ ☆ ☆

GOALS

When you're up to your knees in alligators, it's tough to remember that your original goal was to drain the swamp.

Sportscaster: "I know that your goal was to win, but just when did the turning point come?" Coach: "Right after they played the National Anthem."

You should have at least two goals in life— one to make a little money first, and secondly to make a little money last.

GOLF

A minister had a habit of sneaking out to the back woods golf course to play golf on Sunday afternoons. Gabriel and St. Peter, watching from above, were concerned. One day they decided that the minister should be punished. So St. Peter said to Gabriel, "I'll take care of it next Sunday."

When the minister teed off the ball, it went straight down the fairway and fell into the cup.

Gabriel said to St. Peter, "What kind of punishment is this?"

St. Peter replied, "Who is he going to tell?"

☆ ☆ ☆

I lost only two golf balls last season—I was putting at the time.

☆ ☆ ☆

I did as the pro told me. I kept my head down and my eyes on the ball. But wouldn't you know it? Some darned fool stole my cart.

☆ ☆ ☆

There are 20 million golfers and only 19,999,-999 balls, and that is why, at any given moment, someone is out looking for a lost golf ball.

☆ ☆ ☆

Caddy: "I'm not looking at my watch, sir, this is my compass."

☆ ☆ ☆

Then there was the golfer who was so used to cheating that when he made a hole in one he wrote down zero.

A foursome of golfers always managed to be in by six p.m. One day they were a full hour late. When they came in, the pro inquired, "Whatever happened that you fellows were so late today?"

"Well," replied one, "everything was o.k. until the fourth tee, and then Frank had a stroke and died. After that it was hit the ball, drag Frank, hit the ball, drag Frank."

☆ ☆ ☆

"What is your handicap?"
"My driver, my irons and my putter."

☆ ☆ ☆

"This is the toughest course I ever played on."
Caddy: "Sir, how can you tell? You haven't even been on the course yet."

☆ ☆ ☆

I'm always having great difficulty deciding whether to play golf or go to church on Sunday. For example, last Sunday I had to flip a coin 27 times.

☆ ☆ ☆

Golf is really a stupid game. I'm glad I don't have to play it again until next week.

☆ ☆ ☆

"Reverend, is it a sin to play golf on Sunday?"
"In your case, it's a sin every day."

A lot of ministers don't play golf because they don't have the vocabulary for it.

"How's your daughter's golf?"
"Oh, she's going around in less and less every day."
"Yes, I know, but how's her golf?"

GOOD NEWS — BAD NEWS

A pilot flying a superjet for the first time turned on the intercom in the cockpit and told his passengers that he had both good news and bad news for them. The good news was that they were making real good time, and the bad news was that they were lost.

☆ ☆ ☆

A man was telling his friend how his airplane engine had failed.
"That's bad," replied his friend.
"No, I had a parachute."
"That was good."
"No, it didn't open."
"That was bad."
"No, there was a haystack below."
"That was good."
"No, there was a pitchfork in the haystack."
"That was bad."
"No, I missed it."

☆ ☆ ☆

A fellow jumped out of the top window of a skyscraper, and as he was passing a window half way down, he was overheard to remark, "So far, so good."

☆ ☆ ☆

"I haven't told you about my grandchildren, have I?"
"No, and I appreciate it, too."

☆ ☆ ☆

A young executive to the president of the corporation: "The good news is that we can buy the Empire State Building for $50 million. The bad news is that they want a $1,000 cash down payment."

☆　☆　☆

A bachelor living with his mother was very fond of cats and seldom left the home place. It became necessary for him to make a trip to New York. The day after his arrival he called home and asked the butler how things were, and the butler immediately informed him that his best cat died.

"You spoiled my entire trip," said the bachelor. "You should not have given me such bad news."

"What should I have told you?" asked the butler.

"Well, the first day I called in you might have said that the cat wasn't looking so well. The second day you might have stated that the cat was on the roof, and the third day you might have told me that you had taken the cat to the vet, and on the fourth day, you might have broken the news to me that the cat had died."

"Well, okay, boss, I'll remember to do that the next time you call in."

Then the bachelor said, "Oh, by the way, how is my mother?"

And the butler said, "Well, she's on the roof."

(Story supplied by
Ted Hustad of Wall Drug.)

☆　☆　☆

71

GOVERNMENT

No American wants charity, all he wants are some special concessions from the government disguised under some fair-sounding name such as social justice.

Too bad our grandchildren can't be around to see all the wonderful things we're doing with their money.

Blessed are the young, for they shall inherit the national debt.

Only Americans have fostered the art of being prosperous, though broke.

I'm disturbed by laws designed to prohibit winners from being winners in order to prevent losers from being losers.

Whenever one man gets something without earning it, some other man has to earn something without getting it.

If you think OSHA is a small town in Wisconsin you have another think coming.

☆ ☆ ☆

God gives every bird his food, but he doesn't throw it into the nest.

☆ ☆ ☆

"Who," I inquired of a sharp looking fellow, "will be the next president of the United States?"

"Sir," he said, " if you don't mind, I should like to try four years without one."

☆ ☆ ☆

A young orphan boy who was having some difficult times wrote a letter addressed to God. "Dear God," he said, "I would really appreciate it if you could send me $100 so that my sisters and I can have better food and some clothing." He signed it and sent it to Washington, D. C.

Several months later a letter postmarked Washington arrived with a five dollar bill in it. The little boy sat down and wrote another letter. "Dear God, thanks so much for the $5. But if you don't mind, next time please don't send it through Washington — they deducted $95 for administrative costs."

GROWING OLDER

I'm at that awkward age. Too old to twist and too young to waltz.

Many ills are cured by telling the sick person that the symptoms of his illness are signs of advancing age.

After age 40 you become nothing more than a maintenance problem.

Life begins at 40 and so does arthritis, rheumatism and lumbago.

☆　☆　☆

Grandma no longer wears her nightcap—she drinks it.

☆　☆　☆

There are three things that happen to you when you grow older. First you begin to lose your eyesight, then you tend to forget, and third — I can't remember.

☆　☆　☆

There are three stages to man—the first 20 years he learns, the next 20 he earns, and the next 20 he yearns.

☆　☆　☆

A patient came to see his doctor and said "I think I'm losing my memory."

"How long has this been going on?" inquired the doctor.

"How long has what been going on?" asked the patient.

☆ ☆ ☆

I am in my **early** nineties.

☆ ☆ ☆

There are three ages to all of us. Youth, middle age, and you are looking fine.

☆ ☆ ☆

Three elderly gentlemen were talking. One said, "I remember Teddy Roosevelt."

The second said, "I remember Woodrow Wilson."

And the third said, "I remember Elizabeth Taylor."

"Well," responded one of the guys, "she's not even dead yet."

"Neither am I," said the speaker.

☆ ☆ ☆

"I heard that you had a lovely cake. Did you count the candles?"

"No, I tried, but the heat drove me back."

☆ ☆ ☆

About the time a man begins to wonder what life is all about he sees a pretty girl and starts taking vitamin pills.

☆ ☆ ☆

75

When you no longer need a pillow to play Santa Claus, you're middle-aged.

☆ ☆ ☆

You're not old when your teeth decay,
You're not old when your hair turns gray,
But you're old as sure as the sea is deep
If your head makes dates that your feet can't keep.

☆ ☆ ☆

Well, there's one thing to be said in favor of being over 40. Women are still interested in you, but the army isn't.

☆ ☆ ☆

Though I'll soon be pushing 60,
I'm as solid as a rock,
And a devil at all parties
At least until nine o'clock.

☆ ☆ ☆

My first 75 years have taught me that if you stick around long enough you'll see everything —twice.

—Quincy Howe

☆ ☆ ☆

HIPPIES

A hippie walking down the street with one shoe was asked, "Did you lose a shoe?"

"No," came back the reply, "I found one."

☆　☆　☆

The very first rock festival was staged by David and Goliath.

☆　☆　☆

There's one thing to be said for long hair and beards. They're a boon to people with ugly faces.

☆　☆　☆

At the wedding ceremony, the minister said, "Will one or the other of you please give the ring to the bride?"

☆　☆　☆

An elderly man, seeing a youngster come down the street, turned and addressed a bystander.

"Isn't it goshawful how these girls and boys dress alike? You can't even tell what it is."

"It's a girl," said the bystander.

Whereupon the elderly gentleman asked, "How do you know? Are you her mother?"

"No," retorted the bystander, "I'm her father."

☆　☆　☆

A man and his wife argued about whether four hippies that they were observing were girls. The lady finally approached the group and asked, "Are you sisters?"

"No," one of them responded, "we're not even Catholic."

HISTORY

Reader's Note: General Custer was considered one of this nation's great post-Civil War army generals. His defeat and the total annihilation of his troops at the Battle of the Little Big Horn have precipitated dozens of Custer stories. Here are a few examples:

Custer's last words: "Where in H--- did all these Indians come from?"

General Custer was a well-dressed man. When they found him he was wearing an Arrow shirt.

Many communities in eastern Dakota fail to grow and prosper because Custer, when he went through there, told the citizens, "Don't do anything until I return."

As General Custer fell mortally wounded, he cried out to the soldiers, "Take no prisoners."

So much for the Custer stories—

If our first president, George Washington, was first in war, first in peace, and first in the hearts of his countrymen, why is it that he married a widow?

☆ ☆ ☆

Eisenhower: "I shot 85 at Augusta."
Khrushchev: "That's nothing. I shot 10,000 at Budapest."

☆ ☆ ☆

I was born under the sign of Leo. My mother did not want to miss seeing the end of a Metro-Goldwyn-Mayer picture.

☆ ☆ ☆

If Washington were alive today, he'd be an old man.

☆ ☆ ☆

History repeats itself because we don't listen the first time.

☆ ☆ ☆

If it were not for Thomas Edison we would be watching television by candlelight.

☆ ☆ ☆

Abraham Lincoln was once taken to task by an associate for his attitude toward his enemies.
"Why," he was asked, "do you try to make friends with them? You should try to destroy them."
To which Lincoln replied: "Am I not destroying my enemies when I make them my friends?"

☆ ☆ ☆

HOMETOWN

My town is so small that the only thing we do for excitement is to go over to the depot on Saturdays to see the train come in.

Our library is not very large. People go there mostly to thumb through the Sears Roebuck and Gurney's spring seed catalogs.

Our town is so small that it does not even have a zip code.

A friend of mine comes from a town that is so square that cottage cheese is found in the gourmet section at the supermarket.

A small town is a place where everyone knows whose check is good and whose husband isn't.

☆　☆　☆

I refuse to fly in anything bigger than my home town. When that 747 took off I thought the whole airport was taking off.

☆　☆　☆

I come from a town that has 400 souls—and about the same number of heels.

☆　☆　☆

My hometown is the geographic center of the entire surrounding area.

This is a wonderful town. When I arrived I couldn't speak, I couldn't walk, I scarcely had any hair on my head, and they had to lift me from my bed. I was born here.

Our town was so small that they discontinued bringing in a cleaning lady.

Our town was so small that the last one home at night turned out the street lights.

Not much to see, but what you hear makes up for it.

Ours is a friendly city. If you will check the yellow pages in our phone book you will find that we have more doctors ushering in the newborn than we have undertakers ushering out the dead.

☆　☆　☆

HUNTING

A hunter lost in the wilds of northern Minnesota screamed at his guide, "You told me you were the best guide in Minnesota."

"Yes," replied the guide, "I am, but I think we're in Canada now."

☆ ☆ ☆

Two fellows went duck hunting. One told his new-found friend that he was known to snore at night, and if he did hear him snoring, to simply get up and shake him. Shortly after they turned out the lights, his buddy went over to his bunk and kissed him on the cheek. There was no snoring that night.

☆ ☆ ☆

A sportsman fed his hunting dog marijuana, and now he no longer points, he just waves.

☆ ☆ ☆

An old hunter preparing his own shells rammed in a charge of salt. "Why," asked his hunting buddy, "are you doing that?"

"Well," he said, "when I drop those bucks way out, it keeps the meat from spoiling until I get there."

☆ ☆ ☆

A bird in the hand makes blowing your nose difficult.

☆ ☆ ☆

INFLATION

They call it take home pay because there's no other place you can afford to go with it.

☆ ☆ ☆

I bought stock as a hedge against inflation, and now see what's happened. My hedge got trimmed.

☆ ☆ ☆

The way my weight is going up reminds me of inflation.

☆ ☆ ☆

A man said that his biggest financial problem was at the end of the month when he had too much month left and not enough money.

☆ ☆ ☆

"Give me twenty cents worth of potatoes."
"Why don't you take a whole one?"

☆ ☆ ☆

If you want to teach a child the value of a dollar, you'd better do it quickly.

☆ ☆ ☆

If you think the cost of living is high, just wait until your wife gets your funeral bill.

☆ ☆ ☆

Inflation is now so bad that it takes three to make a pair.

☆ ☆ ☆

It costs more to live today, but I wonder if it is worth more.

☆ ☆ ☆

It's tough to pay $1.50 for a steak, but it's tougher if you pay 99 cents.

☆ ☆ ☆

LAW AND ORDER

Judge: "You were brought in here for drinking."

Defendant: "When do we start, Your Honor?"

☆   ☆   ☆

"Why didn't you try to settle the case out of court?" the judge asked the litigants.

"That's just what we were trying to do when the police came and interfered."

☆   ☆   ☆

There is no arrest for the wicked.

☆   ☆   ☆

The lawyer for the defendant was successful in getting a suspended sentence. They hanged him.

☆   ☆   ☆

If the law is on my side, I hammer on the law.

If the facts are on my side, I hammer on the facts.

If neither the law nor the facts are on my side, I hammer on the table.

☆   ☆   ☆

"I'll give you 30 days or $100," said the judge.

"I'll take the $100," replied the defendant.

☆   ☆   ☆

"I can't understand," said the defendant, "why I should be charged with forgery—I can't even sign my own name."

"You are not charged with signing your own name," replied the judge.

☆ ☆ ☆

"Is this Boyce, Murphy, McDowell, Greenfield, Vickers, Pashby, McDowell and Goldammer?"

"Yes, this is Boyce, Murphy, McDowell, Greenfield, Vickers, Pashby, McDowell and Goldammer."

"I want to talk to Jones."

☆ ☆ ☆

Only lawyers can write documents containing 5,000 or more words and call it a brief.

☆ ☆ ☆

My husband is the most unlucky man I've ever known. He's the only man alive that reported for jury duty and was found guilty.

☆ ☆ ☆

MARRIAGE

Married men have better halves, bachelors have better quarters.

☆ ☆ ☆

"How did you make out in that fight with your wife?"
"Just fine, she came crawling to me on her hands and knees, and said come out from under that bed, you coward."

☆ ☆ ☆

My husband is good at fixing things around the house—like martinis, old-fashioneds, and manhattans.

☆ ☆ ☆

"Who gave you that black eye?"
"My wife."
"I thought she was out of town."
"So did I."

☆ ☆ ☆

You're nobody until somebody loves you and the next thing you know you are a den mother.

☆ ☆ ☆

After a noisy argument, a wife snapped at her husband, "Did you hear my last remark?"
"I certainly hope so," he replied.

☆ ☆ ☆

Most women could be cured of jealousy if they'd just take one good impartial look at their husbands.

☆ ☆ ☆

Let her stay home and wash and iron and cook and clean and take care of the kids. No wife of mine is going to work.

☆ ☆ ☆

A man complained about having had two unhappy marriages. His first wife divorced him and his second one wouldn't.

☆ ☆ ☆

A second marriage is a triumph of hope over experience.

☆ ☆ ☆

He is not chasing women any more. First of all, he's lost his interest, second, his inclination, and third, his wind.

☆ ☆ ☆

My wife must be a good cook. Even the truck drivers are stopping at our place to eat.

☆ ☆ ☆

The guy that said that talk was cheap probably never said, "I do."

☆ ☆ ☆

I'm not as old as I look. I married young, I worried a lot, and I'm moulting prematurely.

☆ ☆ ☆

"I've been married for thirty years, and it hasn't been half bad."

"How so?"

"I've been gone half the time."

☆　☆　☆

My wife and I have had a very simple relationship down through the years. I rule the roost and she rules the rooster.

☆　☆　☆

I proposed to my wife in the garage and couldn't back out.

☆　☆　☆

Marriage is like a violin. After the beautiful music the strings are still attached.

☆　☆　☆

Marriage is a wonderful thing. It's the living together afterwards that causes all of the difficulties.

☆　☆　☆

Dear, don't expect the first few meals to be very good. It takes time to find the right restaurants.

☆　☆　☆

A running mate is a husband who dared to talk back.

☆　☆　☆

Remember after marriage, what's done is done.

☆　☆　☆

The biggest cause of divorce is marriage.

☆ ☆ ☆

I married for better and for worse — she couldn't do any worse and I couldn't do any better.

☆ ☆ ☆

"Why did you get married?"
"What else was there to do?"

☆ ☆ ☆

I try to argue with my wife but every time I do words fail me.

☆ ☆ ☆

MATHEMATICS

A Missouri farmer passed away and left seventeen mules to his three sons. The instructions left in the will said that the oldest boy was to get 1/2, the second eldest 1/3, and the youngest 1/9. The three sons, recognizing the difficulty of dividing seventeen mules into these fractions, began to argue. The uncle heard about the argument, hitched up his mule and drove out to settle the matter. He added his mule to the 17, making 18. The eldest son therefore got 1/2 or nine; the second got 1/3 or six; and the youngest got 1/9 or two. Adding up 9, 6, and 2 equals 17. The uncle, having settled the argument, hitched up his mule and drove home.

☆ ☆ ☆

Dad, I can explain the poor grade I got in math. The batteries in my calculator went dead.

☆ ☆ ☆

MEDICINE

We have a doctor in our town that has so much charm and personality that when he takes a woman's pulse, he automatically subtracts 10 points for his own personality.

A lady called her doctor in the middle of the night inquiring how much he charged for a house call and how much for an office call. The doctor told her that a house call was $10 and an office call was $5.

She then replied, "I'll see you in your office in about thirty minutes."

☆ ☆ ☆

I have a strange doctor. Last year I had walking pneumonia and he charged me by the mile.

☆ ☆ ☆

A man went to the hospital to get a cardiogram. After the cardiogram had been taken, he was given a sheet of paper with a whole bunch of jiggly lines on it. He took it home and put it into his player piano and it played back, "Nearer My God to Thee".

☆ ☆ ☆

He went to Phoenix for his sinus—finally got it after ten years.

☆ ☆ ☆

A well-adjusted person is one whose intake of pep pills just overbalances his intake of tranquilizers, leaving enough energy for his weekly trip to the psychiatrist.

Addressing his students, the medical professor said, "Now notice how the muscle of the patient's leg is contracted until it is now much shorter than the other. Therefore, he limps. Now, students, what would you do in such circumstances?"

Replied one of the students, "I would limp, too."

☆ ☆ ☆

You've got another one of those nasty colds. It's too bad you don't have pneumonia, we know how to cure that.

☆ ☆ ☆

A practical nurse is one who marries a rich patient.

"Cheer up," said the doctor, "I've had the same thing myself."

"But you didn't have the same doctor," replied the patient.

An ulcer is a pain in the neck that has localized itself in the stomach.

☆ ☆ ☆

You get ulcers not from what you eat, but from what's eating you.

☆ ☆ ☆

Virus is a Latin word used by doctors to mean, "Your guess is as good as mine."

☆　☆　☆

"Doctor, if the pain in my right leg is caused by old age, why doesn't my left leg hurt—it's the same age."

☆　☆　☆

A patient who had been informed that his illness was terminal joined the Communist Party. When asked why, he replied, "It's better that one of them should go."

☆　☆　☆

MEETINGS

If the next time each four of you will bring a fifth, we'll have a livelier meeting.

Many a man goes to a convention in a state of confusion, returns the same way, but, we trust, on a higher level.

Meetings and conventions are functions which one attends to learn things he already knows, but which he does not have time to put in practice because there are so many meetings and conventions to attend.

A meeting is a collection of individuals who individually can do nothing, but who get together and collectively decide that nothing can be done.

Taking your wife to a convention is like taking the game warden on a hunting trip.

MEMBERSHIP DRIVES

We had a membership drive last week and drove out ten members.

The Communist Party in Russia had a membership drive. The rules were as follows: Any Communist who could recruit a new member would no longer have to pay dues. If he got two members, he would be permitted to leave the party, and if he recruited three members he would receive a certificate stating that he had never belonged in the first place.

Once I had joined the organization and paid my dues, I inquired as to what my privileges were.

Back came the answer, "You can pay dues again next year."

MEN

The average woman soon discovers that her ideal man isn't real and her real man isn't ideal.

☆ ☆ ☆

When men get too old to set bad examples, they sit around dishing out good advice.

☆ ☆ ☆

Man is the only animal that can be skinned more than once.

☆ ☆ ☆

Before he was married, he had three theories on children—now he has three children and no more theories.

☆ ☆ ☆

The modern man is a person who drives a mortgaged car on a bond-financed highway with gas purchased on a credit card.

☆ ☆ ☆

She's my type—a woman.

☆ ☆ ☆

Arsonists are not the only guys who get in trouble when playing around with fire.

☆ ☆ ☆

You don't need to lead man into temptation, he can usually find it on his own.

☆ ☆ ☆

MILITARY

Once I knew a mean Army officer who was rotten to the corps.

☆ ☆ ☆

"I suppose after I get discharged," said the tough old squad sergeant, "you'll all be waiting in line to spit on my grave."

"No, sir, sarge," replied one of the privates, "once I'm out of the army, I'll never stand in line again."

☆ ☆ ☆

The draft board has classified me 5-F. I will be sent overseas in case our country is invaded.

☆ ☆ ☆

Near the end of World War II, an army general came to review the troops in western Europe. Two privates had been positioned to open the door of the car. As the general alighted from the front seat, the first private stepped up and kicked him in the pants. The second private, standing near the rear door, took one step forward and also kicked the general.

This episode resulted in a court martial hearing. When the first private was asked why he had kicked the general, he said he really didn't know, that it was just an impulsive thing.

They then asked the second private his reason. "Well, sir," he responded, "when I saw my buddy kick the general, I thought the war was over."

☆ ☆ ☆

If you think old soldiers fade away, you ought to see my husband trying to get into his old uniform.

☆ ☆ ☆

The war for the Japanese was going very badly. To have any chance of holding back the Americans, the Japanese air force had to resort to the use of kamikaze or suicide pilots. At the initial briefing there were some new recruits. The officer in charge told the potential new young kamikaze pilots that when they went in to make that final kill on that American ship that they should think about the wonderful deed that they were doing for their fatherland. When they got all through, he said, "Are there any questions?"

In the back of the room a young farm recruit said, "Yes, officer, are you out of your cotton-picking mind?"

☆ ☆ ☆

The young recruit was going through the process of having a physical examination. When the doctor had completed the examination, he said, "Do you see that bottle on the shelf over there? I'm going to need a specimen."

"From here?" shot back the recruit.

☆ ☆ ☆

My son must have a lot of untidy officers in his regiment. He's always writing about having to clean up the officers' mess.

☆ ☆ ☆

The way to increase our military strength abroad tenfold is to bring home our soldiers and arm our tourists.

The Russians have a new submarine. It can surface and resubmerge in 22 seconds. We sure must take our hats off to the Russians, especially those left standing on the deck.

After college, one young man became a general in the army, the other a priest. Years later, at a railroad depot, the priest, seeing his former classmate, said, "Hey, bellboy, when does the next train leave?"

"Madam," shot back the general, "in your condition, it won't make much difference."

MONEY

Money won't make you happy, it will just keep you comfortable while you're unhappy.

☆ ☆ ☆

I would like to open a joint bank account with someone who has money.

☆ ☆ ☆

I'm very proud of the fact that I've never been overdrawn at my bank—just underdeposited.

☆ ☆ ☆

Rich or poor, it's always nice to have money.

☆ ☆ ☆

A Texas banker came up to our town and wrote a check on a local bank, and the bank bounced.

☆ ☆ ☆

If you count all of your assets, you will always show a profit.

☆ ☆ ☆

A loan officer in the bank told the president, "I've never made a bad loan. Of course," he said, "some went bad."

☆ ☆ ☆

A branch manager is a loan officer up a tree.

☆ ☆ ☆

The Grand Canyon was created by a Scotch-man who dropped a nickel into a gopher hole.

Money is not important. Henry Ford had millions and never owned a Cadillac.

The new two dollar bills make buck-passing twice as difficult.

MORALITY

She was the self-appointed guardian of the village morals. Her chief complaint was the construction worker who parked his wheelbarrow at either the local tavern or in front of the local house of ill repute. Upon hearing the complaint, the man stifled all further complaints by leaving his wheelbarrow in front of the complaining lady's house overnight.

☆ ☆ ☆

The husband came home with a big gash over his eyebrow, and his wife inquired, "What happened to you?"

"I bit myself," he replied.

"Impossible," she said.

"No, it wasn't, I had to stand on a chair to do it."

☆ ☆ ☆

When coming up the stairs one evening, quite inebriated, the husband fell over backwards and broke the bottle of liquor that he was carrying. Not wishing his wife to know what had happened, he went to the bathroom to make the necessary repairs. Next morning when he woke up, his wife said, "Well, you came home drunk again."

"No," he said, "whatever would make you think so?"

"Well," she said, "if you weren't drunk, why is all that adhesive tape on the mirror in the bathroom?"

☆ ☆ ☆

A lady was having real problems with her husband coming home drunk almost every night. She always met him at the door with a tongue lashing. In visiting with some of her neighbors, they told her that she was taking the wrong approach in dealing with her husband's problems.

"When he comes home next time," they told her, "have a sandwich ready for him and treat him very nicely."

She followed her friends' instructions. When her husband came home, she said, "I'm so happy to see you, dear, why don't we go in the kitchen and have a sandwich and visit a little bit."

He agreed.

Finally she said, "Let's go on upstairs to bed."

"Yes," he said, "we might just as well because when I get home I'm going to catch heck anyway."

Dull men and dull women seem to have all the fun.

MORTALITY

The applicant was asked what caused the death of his parents. He replied, "I don't recall, but I don't think it was anything serious."

A man applying for the position of insurance agent was asked what he thought was the normal mortality rate in the area to be served by the insurance company.
He replied, "I really don't know, but I believe it averages about one per person."

Why is it that insurance people always talk about death benefits.

In the South, morticians are called Southern planters.

MOTIVATION

The young man had a job with a company that required him to work the swing shift, from four in the afternoon until midnight. In going home after work, it was always necessary for him to walk around a cemetery that separated his home and his place of employment. One night when he was very tired, he decided to cut across the cemetery. On entering he discovered that there was a beaten path. It being very dark, he kept his feet right in the path, but he didn't know that a new grave had been dug in the center of the path, and of course he fell into it.

At first he was not too concerned, but when he realized that he could not get out because the hole was too deep, he became somewhat hysterical. Ultimately in complete exhaustion he sat down in the corner of the grave and fell asleep. Shortly thereafter the same fate befell another employee. He too went through the same antics of trying to get out. When he was just about to the exhaustion point the first employee woke up and shouted, "YOU CAN'T GET OUT OF HERE."

But he did.

MUSIC AND SONGS

He went out fit as a fiddle, but came home tight as a drum.

☆ ☆ ☆

Tonight we're going to sing three special numbers:
"If you know Susie like I know Susie, you'll go out with Gertrude", and the second one will be, "I tried to look into her eyes, but they were too far apart."
And the last one will be, "Get out of the wheat field, Grandma, you're going against the grain."

☆ ☆ ☆

Next we will have a medley of three songs, one right after another.

☆ ☆ ☆

Modern dance music sure is different. I dropped a tray of dishes and three couples got up to dance.

☆ ☆ ☆

I can yodel but not out loud.

☆ ☆ ☆

OVERDOING

A young Catholic girl came home and told her mother excitedly that she had found a young man that she would like to marry. He was handsome, young, intelligent and his parents had a lot of money. There was only one thing wrong, the young man was not Catholic. The mother then told her to work real hard on this young man and convert him to their religion.

After some period of time the young daughter came home in tears and told her mother that there was not going to be a wedding.

"Why not?" asked the mother. "Did you not work hard to try to convert the young man to our faith?"

"Yes, Mom, I did. But I must have overdone it. He has decided to become a priest."

OPTIMIST - PESSIMIST '

An optimist looks at a glass half-filled with water and says it's half full. The pessimist looking at the same glass says it is half empty.

☆　☆　☆

A man who had been condemned to die was brought before the king for final review and disposition. The defendant pleaded that he wanted to live and the king said, "I'll make you a proposition. If you teach my horse how to fly within one year, I'll set you free."

"Agreed," said the defendant.

"You're a fool," said his cellmates.

"No, I'm not," he shot back.

"How do you figure?" they asked him.

"Well," he said, "let's look at the odds. They just might be on my side. In a year," he said, "the king may die, the horse may die, or I may die, and then there's always the outside possibility that I will teach that horse how to fly."

☆　☆　☆

The optimist invented the airplane and the pessimist the parachute.

☆　☆　☆

All people smile in the same language.

☆　☆　☆

I feel like a snapdragon—no snap and everything draggin'.

☆　☆　☆

A gentleman was found sitting on the steps of the county courthouse on a Monday morning. When an employee arrived, he inquired of the gentleman why he was there so early. "I've just come to see when my marriage license expires."

☆ ☆ ☆

A pessimist is one who has financed an optimist.

☆ ☆ ☆

The man living in an agricultural community kept telling everyone how terrible things were. It wasn't going to rain, there weren't going to be any crops, and the winter was going to be an extremely cold one. He was always a grouch. When folks saw him walking up one side of the street, they would automatically take the other side. One day one of the local residents went to the hospital with a heart attack. The pessimist thought that he ought to go see him. When he got there he found his friend lying under an oxygen tent. "That's too bad," said the pessimist, "that you had a heart attack. But that's the way life is." This went on for some period of time and he finally concluded, "and now you're probably going to die."

And the patient under the oxygen tent simply responded, "I sure will, unless you take your foot off the oxygen tube!"

PHILOSOPHY

Troubles that are shared are halved; joys that are shared are doubled.

☆　☆　☆

Often your reasons are wrong, but your thinking is right. So do it.

☆　☆　☆

There is a German proverb that says, "It takes a great many shovelfuls to bury the truth."

☆　☆　☆

Always tell the truth because then you don't have to remember what you said.

☆　☆　☆

Dreams cannot come true if you oversleep.

☆　☆　☆

Diogenes, upon returning from his search for the honest man, was asked, "Any luck?" "Yes," he replied, "I still have my lantern."

☆　☆　☆

A young man asked Socrates if he should get married, and Socrates replied, "By all means, young man, get married. If you find a good wife you'll be happy. If you find a poor one, you'll be a philosopher."

☆　☆　☆

Socrates said that if every man and every woman would have to bring all of their problems and put them into a common heap from which each would have to take an equal portion, each would be willing to take his own and depart.

☆ ☆ ☆

If you come to the end of a perfect day, check again.

☆ ☆ ☆

If you dance with a grizzly bear, let him lead.

☆ ☆ ☆

Show me a man with both feet on the ground, and I'll show you a man that can't put on his trousers.

☆ ☆ ☆

Teach your son to cut his own wood. It will warm him twice.　　　　—Mark Twain

☆ ☆ ☆

The greatest thing in life is to trust and be trusted.

☆ ☆ ☆

It is better to give away your money while you're alive. It doesn't take any great generosity to give it away when you're dead.

☆ ☆ ☆

The mill will not grind with water that is past.

☆ ☆ ☆

Everyone in the world is tolerant if you ask him.
☆ ☆ ☆

If we can't be thankful for what we receive, we should be thankful for what we escape.

☆ ☆ ☆

We make a living by what we get, but we make a life by what we give.

☆ ☆ ☆

Wisdom is knowing what to do next.

☆ ☆ ☆

It is never safe to look into the future with eyes of fear.

☆ ☆ ☆

The next time you think life is not worth living, stop and think of the alternative.

☆ ☆ ☆

Men who do things that count never stop to count them.

☆ ☆ ☆

Nothing becomes real until it becomes personal.

☆ ☆ ☆

POLITICS

Walking candidates are those that find that these are the times that test men's soles.

☆ ☆ ☆

I like political jokes unless they get elected.

☆ ☆ ☆

The invitation to a political fund-raising dinner said, "$100 per plate (roquefort dressing 25 cents extra)."

☆ ☆ ☆

Many politicians have presence of mind, but absence of thought.

☆ ☆ ☆

"I'm very patriotic," said the candidate. "I zipcode all my mail."

☆ ☆ ☆

There are three types of politicians: those that cannot lie, those that cannot tell the truth, and those that cannot tell the difference.

☆ ☆ ☆

Churchill got into a heated debate with a lady member of the Parliament. The lady became so irate with Churchill that she told him that if he were her husband, she would poison his tea. Churchill replied, "If you were my wife, I would drink it."

☆ ☆ ☆

"What do you think of our two candidates?"
"Well, I'm glad only one can be elected."

☆ ☆ ☆

A constituent told the candidate, "I wouldn't vote for you if you were St. Peter."

"If I were St. Peter," replied the candidate, "you couldn't vote for me—you wouldn't be in the same precinct."

Three rather worldly gentlemen were discussing what it meant to be important. The first one said that you would be important if you were invited to the White House for a talk with the president.

"No," said the second one, "you'd be really important if, while visiting the president, he received a call on the hot line and the president would not answer it."

"Still wrong," said the third. "You'd really be important if you're talking with the president when the hot line rings, and he answers it and says, 'It's for you.'"

☆ ☆ ☆

An appreciative candidate in the upper midwest put an ad into the local newspaper which read, "I want to thank the 400 citizens who encouraged me to run for office. I want to extend a special thanks to the 800 friends that promised to vote for me. I also want to thank the 200 that assured me that they did vote for me, and finally, a real vote of thanks to the 75 people who actually cast ballots for me in the recent election."

Two men flying on an airplane were discussing their imminent homecoming. Said the first, "I'm just out of prison and I know it's going to be tough."

Said the second, "I know what you mean, I'm just getting home from Congress."

"You are my second choice."
"Who is your first?"
"Whoever announces his candidacy next."

My friend is running for Mayor. He's never been a grafter. All he wants is a chance.

And then there was a fellow who liked the off-year elections better because his conscience did not bother him as much for not voting.

I don't belong to any organized political party, I am a Republican (Democrat).

I will run a clean campaign unless I can find something really juicy on my opponent.

☆ ☆ ☆

"Do you partake of intoxicating beverages?" inquired the constituent.

"Is that an inquiry or an invitation?" responded the candidate.

☆ ☆ ☆   117

You can lead a Democrat (Republican) to Washington but you cannot make him think.

☆ ☆ ☆

You can tell a Republican (Democrat), but you can't tell him much.

☆ ☆ ☆

If re-elected I will promise to fulfill the promises that I made in the last campaign.

☆ ☆ ☆

My opponent is standing on his platform because he is afraid that someone will try to examine it.

☆ ☆ ☆

"In the recent election, where did the turning point come?"
"Right after I threw my hat into the ring."

☆ ☆ ☆

HOW TO TELL REPUBLICANS FROM DEMOCRATS: Republicans give their clothes to the less fortunate; Democrats wear theirs. Republicans employ exterminators; Democrats step on bugs. Democrats buy most of the books that have been banned somewhere; Republicans form censorship committees and read them as a group. Republican boys date Democrat girls —they plan to marry Republican girls but they feel they're entitled to a little fun first. Republicans sleep in twin beds, some even in separate rooms; that's why there are more Democrats. (From the Congressional Record, author unknown.)

☆ ☆ ☆

Both Theodore Roosevelt and John Kennedy have been credited with the following: The credit belongs to the man actually in the arena whose face is marred by dust and sweat and blood . . . who knows the great enthusiasm . . . the great devotion to duty . . . and spends himself in a worthy cause.

Who at best if he wins knows the thrill of high achievement, and if he fails, at least he fails while daring greatly . . . His place shall never be with those cold and timid souls who know neither victory nor defeat.

"You'll get the vote of every thinking person."
"Fine—but I need a majority."

Those are my views. If you don't like them, I'll change them.

Quitters never win and winners never quit.

A man who runs for re-election is basically honest, which means he didn't get his hand in there the first time.

☆ ☆ ☆

I don't care who you are voting for, get out of my shower.

☆ ☆ ☆

A politician is a man full of promise.

☆ ☆ ☆

In this campaign I want you to know that my wife is not a side issue.

☆ ☆ ☆

Some politicians can't remember if they were born in a manger or a log cabin.

☆ ☆ ☆

Before Columbus discovered America there were no taxes, no Watergate, no Democrats, no Republicans, no energy crises, no TV commercials, plenty of fish, no pollution, and women did all the work. —And now we have politicians who want to improve on that?

☆ ☆ ☆

At a cabinet meeting, Franklin Roosevelt told of an American Marine who had been terribly depressed because he had not killed even one of the enemy. He brought his case to his superior officer who told the Marine to go to the top of the hill and shout, "To hell with Emperor Hirohito," to bring the Japs out of hiding. The Marine did as he was told.

Immediately a Japanese soldier emerged out of the jungle and shouted, "To hell with President Roosevelt."

"But," said the Marine, "I simply could not kill a Republican."

☆ ☆ ☆

What are the three major parties?
Democrat, Republican, and cocktail.

☆ ☆ ☆

I'm a confused Independent.

☆ ☆ ☆

Political ignorance: When you don't know something and someone finds it out.

☆ ☆ ☆

Primary: The political dating game.

☆ ☆ ☆

POLLS

A lion was walking through the forest taking a poll to determine who was the greatest among all the wildlife animals. When he saw the hippopotamus, he inquired, "Who is king of the forest?"

"You are," said the hippopotamus.

Next he met a giraffe. "Who is the king of the forest?" he inquired.

"You are," said the giraffe.

Next he met the elephant. He gave him a good rap on the knee and said, "And who is king of the forest?"

Whereupon the elephant picked him up in his trunk and swung him against the tree. As the lion slid down, brushing himself off, he said, "You don't have to get so mad just because you don't know the right answer."

A psychologist took a poll surveying just how people sat in their tubs. He discovered that out of a hundred people, 99 sat facing the faucets. Only one sat facing away from the faucets. They asked the lone man why and he said, "Very simple, I have no plug for my tub."

POPULATION CONTROL

The reason California has earthquakes is because so many of its citizens forget to take their earth control pills.

Then there was the secretary who dropped her birth control pill in the xerox machine and it would not reproduce.

As the last member of a family of 12, I have mixed emotions about this business of population control.

The government is concerned about the population explosion, and the population is concerned about government explosion.

If your parents didn't have children, chances are you won't either.

Emcees are not made—that's why some people advocate birth control.

I came from a large family—never slept alone until I was married.

Population control
   Would be more effective
If it could be made
   Retroactive.

"Do you know what the best birth control pill in the world is?"
"No."
"That's it."

POVERTY

We were so poor that we could afford rickets in only one leg.

☆　☆　☆

We were so poor that Dad would give us a dime for not eating.

☆　☆　☆

Times were so tough that when we hitch-hiked, we'd take a ride either way.

☆　☆　☆

The poor seek food, the rich seek appetites.

☆　☆　☆

Times were so tough that when Dad said grace, he kept both hands over the butter plate.

☆　☆　☆

We were so poor I remember my mother serving five leathery little porkchops for the ten of us. But I shouldn't complain—the two I got weren't too bad.

☆　☆　☆

We were so poor we were made in Japan.

☆　☆　☆

My Dad couldn't wait for the depression of 1929. He started ours in 1928.

☆　☆　☆

During the depression, the fellow ordered a bowl of soup in the restaurant, and as he was about to eat it, a fly fell in the soup. So he carefully fished it out, and holding the fly's right wing between his right thumb and forefinger, and the fly's left wing between his left thumb and forefinger, he said, "Now, darnit, spit it out."

RELATIVES

A relative is the kin you love to touch.

I have so many relatives that they're coming out of the woodwork.

"I took the deduction," said the taxpayer to the Internal Revenue agent, "because my relatives are an organized charity."

A large family was finally able to move into a more spacious home. Sometime later an uncle asked his nephew, "How do you like your new house?"

"Just fine," replied the lad. "My brother and I have our own rooms, and so do my sisters. But poor Mom, she's still stuck in the same room with Dad."

RELIGION

Item in a church bulletin: Our minister is leaving the church this Sunday. Will you please send in a small donation. The congregation wants to give him a little momentum.

A young man worked for a lumber company. He was a very good man, but he had one bad habit. Each night when he finished work he would put a piece of lumber into his truck. Soon he had a big pile of lumber. Finally his conscience began to bother him. And being Catholic he went to see his priest and confessed everything. Father listened very intently and then said, "Young man, you have done something very, very serious. You're going to have to make a novena. Do you know what a novena is?"

"No, Father," he said, "I sure don't, but if you've got the plans, I've got the lumber."

A Quaker was milking a cow when she switched her tail, hitting him directly in the eye. This disturbed him greatly. So he got up, and facing the cow, he said, "Thou knowest that I'm a Quaker, that I cannot smite thee, but what thou don't know is that I can sell thee to my friend who is not a Quaker, and he can beat the holy —— out of thee."

☆　☆　☆

The pastor said there were 250 sins, so one of the parishioners wrote in for the list.

☆　☆　☆

A young man had just been ordained. He worked hard on his first sermon trying to make a good impression. As he leaped into the pulpit he shouted, "BEHOLD, I COME," and then his throat went dry and he could speak no more. So he stepped out of the pulpit, waited a few seconds, and then tried again. And again he said, "BEHOLD, I COME."

Again his throat went dry, so he tried a third time with all the vigor and strength that he could muster, "BEHOLD, I COME," but he overshot the pulpit and landed on the lap of a lady in the front row.

As he got up to apologize, the lady said, "You need not do so, Reverend, after all, I had two warnings."

☆　☆　☆

The Sunday School lesson was on honesty. The teacher inquired of his class, "Would all of those of you who read the 35th chapter of Matthew raise your right hand?"

A number of them raised their hands.

And then he said. "You are the ones I want to talk to. There is no 35th Chapter of Matthew."

☆　☆　☆

Little Jimmy was attending his first Sunday School class. "Do you say your prayers before eating?" inquired his teacher.

"I don't have to," responded the boy, "my mother is a good cook."

☆　☆　☆

The visiting pastor put fifty cents in the collection plate as it was passed. As he departed from the church after the service, the head usher handed him the collection plate and stated that it was customary for his church to give the pastor the entire offering. When he looked in the plate, there he saw his own fifty cent piece. The moral of this story is, that had he put more into it, he would have gotten more out of it.

The church was having trouble raising its annual budget. A member of the congregation, an electrician, came up with a great idea. He said, "We will wire all of the seats, and then when our chairman of fund raising asks for pledges on Sunday morning, we will follow something like the following procedure. Will all those who will pledge $5 per week please stand up? And then the electrician will punch the $5 button."

They went through this procedure up to what they felt would be the maximum limits of some to pledge. After the congregation had been dismissed, in the back row they found that the only Scotch member of the congregation had been electrocuted.

"You must repent or die," said the minister. Whereupon a visitor to the church said, "I'm sure glad I'm not a member of this church."

If all the men in our church were laid end to end, they would sleep more comfortably.

☆ ☆ ☆

Sign on a church bulletin board. If you don't like what you hear on a given Sunday, your sins will be cheerfully refunded.

A man who had been living a high life decided that he wanted to repent. So he went to the Baptist Church and asked to be baptized. The minister performed the rites of immersion in front of the congregation. When he came up out of the water the newly baptized man said that he felt so great that he was going to give ten per cent of everything he earned to the church. Whereupon the reverend replied, "We have a tither in our tank."

A minister had a habit of preaching on whatever verse he happened to point his finger to when he opened the Bible. This particular Sunday morning, he opened the Bible and the finger pointed to the verse, "And Judas went out and hanged himself." He was not in such a pessimistic mood so he violated his procedure and thumbed through an additional few pages of the Bible and dropped his finger and it read, "Go ye, and do likewise."

Some families think that Sunday morning church is like a convention, each family sending one delegate.

☆ ☆ ☆

I'm a widower—the Lord took my wife away, but He will regret it.

☆ ☆ ☆

Asked to draw a picture of the biblical flight into Egypt, a boy drew a plane with four people in it flying toward Egypt. Three of the passengers had halos.

"Who are they?" inquired the Sunday School teacher.

"They are Jesus, Joseph and Mary," replied the boy.

"And who is the one without the halo?"

"That is Pontius the Pilot," replied the boy.

☆ ☆ ☆

Three nuns were each given $100. The first nun said that she wanted to give hers to some Catholic youth organization; the next stipulated that hers might go to a child welfare organization; and the third nun said she was going out on the street and give it to the first person she ran into that really looked like he needed it.

She went down the street and the first guy she met was an elderly fellow who was dressed in very shabby clothes, so she thrust the $100 bill into the palm of his hand. She became choked up and really couldn't say anything except, "Godspeed."

Two days later this fellow appeared at the convent and said that he wanted to see the nun that had given him a $100 bill. He tried to describe her and said that he really didn't know how to describe a nun but, anyway, he surmised that it was Sister Helena.

When she got to the door, the man said he was so grateful for what she had done the other day that he went to the races and Godspeed had come in first.

And he gave her $800.00.

☆ ☆ ☆

A minister, in administering the confirmation rites for an elderly new member, asked, "Do you repent of the devil and all of his ways?"

The member replied, "In my position, I can't afford to antagonize anyone."

"Doctor, is there anything you can do to cure me of snoring?" asked the gentleman.

The doctor asked, "Does it disturb your wife?"

"No," replied the client, "it only embarrasses my wife. It's the rest of the congregation that's disturbed."

☆ ☆ ☆

RESTAURANT

"Waiter, bring me some of your spumoni vermicelli that's on the menu."

"Sorry, sir, that's the proprietor."

In the last century America was known as the melting pot. Today it has become the pressure cooker.

Don't just stand there, help stamp out home cooking.

Sign in a restaurant window: If you don't eat here, we'll both starve.

☆ ☆ ☆

Let's put out a tranquilizing cheese for folks who like quiet parties.

☆ ☆ ☆

Customer: "What's that fly doing in my soup?"

Waitress: "It looks like he's doing the backstroke."

☆ ☆ ☆

He may not be the lousiest chef in the world, but I can tell you one thing — there are no ants in his kitchen.

☆ ☆ ☆

Don't criticize a man for flirting with the waitress — he may be playing for big steaks.

☆　☆　☆

The public health service reports that there are at least 10 million overweight people in the United States. Those are round figures, of course.

☆　☆　☆

In a coffee shop a traveling salesman summoned a waitress and gave her his order, "Two eggs and fry them very hard, two slices of toast burned black, and a cup of cold coffee."

"I can't do that for you," the waitress said.

"The heck you can't," replied the customer. "You did it for me yesterday."

☆　☆　☆

The wife said to her husband at a buffet dinner, "That's the third time you've gone back for more chicken. Doesn't that embarrass you?"

"No, dear," he said, "I keep telling them I'm getting it for you."

☆　☆　☆

"Waiter, please bring me a clean soup bowl. The bottom of this one is wet."

"That's your soup, sir."

SALESMEN

A formula for success in making house to house calls is after knocking and the lady comes to the door, you inquire, "Miss, is your mother in?"

Always tell me why it can be done, never tell me why it cannot be done.

Henry Ford was bound to succeed. First, he built an automobile without a reverse in it, and second, the harder he worked the luckier he got.

☆ ☆ ☆

I've been leading a dog's life, traveling from pole to pole.

☆ ☆ ☆

A salesman that keeps thinking about eating marshmallows might wake up some morning and find his pillow is gone.

☆ ☆ ☆

Living a double life will get you nowhere twice as fast.

☆ ☆ ☆

Even if you're on the right track, you can be run over if you just sit there.

A town located a mile off the main highway west of the Paul Revere town of Boston was having great difficulties. The city fathers met time and time again to revive the community's economy. But all to no avail.

One day a young man showed up and told the city fathers, "I have the solution."

"What is it?" they inquired.

"We must put a billboard up out at the junction of the highway."

They replied, "We already have a billboard there."

"In that case," said the salesman, "we'll have to change the copy."

The salesman was authorized to change the copy, and after he did business began to boom. On the billboard he put these words: THIS IS THE ROAD THAT PAUL REVERE WOULD HAVE TAKEN HAD HE COME THIS WAY.

☆ ☆ ☆

The hotel clerk told the salesman that there were no more rooms with bath, and would he mind sharing a bath with another man.

"No," said the salesman, "not as long as he stays at his end of the tub."

☆ ☆ ☆

The greatest salesman that I ever heard of was a milking machine salesman. He went out to see a farmer who had only one cow, sold him two milking machines and took the cow as a downpayment.

☆ ☆ ☆

You cannot automate a salesman.

☆ ☆ ☆

The man who rolls up his sleeves seldom loses his shirt.

Why complain about your troubles? They're the reason for half your income.

Everything is difficult the first time.

We don't want any yes men around here—agreed?

The average guy is as close to the bottom as he is to the top.

You can get business by asking for it.

☆ ☆ ☆

Selling is timing.

☆ ☆ ☆

Do you know the difference between love and rape?
Salesmanship.

Blessed is the salesman who travels in circles for he shall be called a wheel.

The greatest underdeveloped territory in the world is under your own hat.

☆ ☆ ☆

Eighty-five per cent of all successful sales come after the fifth call.

Nothing happens until a sale is made.

We're going to have another sales contest. The first prize will be that you get to keep your job.

It's not your aptitude, but rather your attitude that determines your altitude in life.

SECRETARIES

The boss said to his secretary, "You should have been here at eight o'clock this morning." "Why?" asked the secretary. "What happened?"

This is the earliest you've ever been late.

I don't have a private secretary because I don't have a private office.

My secretary doesn't smoke, drink or gamble —her other bad habits don't leave her enough time.

The successful secretary is the pretty young thing who can think like a man, look like a lady, and work like a dog.

Some Congressmen believe in life, liberty, and the pursuit of secretaries.

SERVICE

The best way to forget your own problems is to help someone else.

Joys that are shared are doubled.
Troubles that are shared are halved.

Service to others is the rent we pay for the privilege of living on this planet.

Let us be kind to one another—we are all fighting a tough battle.

There are three types of people in every town—those that live in the town, those that live off the town, and those that live for the town.

The fun in life comes in the doing.

The best exercise is to bend down and help someone up.

SMOKING

I've read so much about the bad effec
smoking that I've decided to quit reading ———

☆　☆　☆

A fellow showed up for work with his
all bandaged up.
"Whatever happened?"
"Last night I was downtown getting s
cigars and a clumsy old fool stepped on
hand."

☆　☆　☆

Tobacco companies have discovered a
to use cheese for cigarette filters. The sm
now comes through fresh and breezy and
a trifle cheesy.

☆　☆　☆

SPEAKER

I'm going to use the Vitamin B approach—
I'm going to be brief, then I'm going to be
seated, and then I'm going to be gone.

☆ ☆ ☆

When talking be as brief as when you are
making a will. The fewer the words, the less
chances for litigation.

☆ ☆ ☆

Sometimes we forget to turn off the sound
when our minds go blank.

☆ ☆ ☆

Do not engage mouth until brain is in gear.

☆ ☆ ☆

"Do you believe in free speech?"
"I most certainly do."
"Then why don't you come to our town next
week and give us a free talk at the Rotary
Club?"

☆ ☆ ☆

I've had a request__but I will speak anyway.

☆ ☆ ☆

You've been a wonderful audience, you
stayed.

☆ ☆ ☆

Apple pie and speeches are improved with
shortening.

☆ ☆ ☆

There is an old proverb that says, "If I listen, I have the advantage. If I speak, others have it."

If you are a poor speaker, don't tell everyone. They will find out soon enough.

I'm not going to bore you with a long speech, I can do it with a short one.

Flattery does not hurt one so long as he doesn't inhale it.

If you ask me how long it will take to prepare a 15 minute speech, my answer will be six hours. If you ask me how long it would take me to prepare a two hour speech, I'd tell you that I was ready now.

Some speakers are good. Some speakers are lousy. I'm good and lousy.

Mine is a low budget talk.

I guess I'm going to return for another speech. I just got a letter saying it would be a cold night before they would have me back again.

☆ ☆ ☆

Gladstone said that a speech need not be eternal to be immortal.

It's un-American not to speak when invited to do so.

He might not be the best speaker, but he will stay with you the longest.

Our speaker needs no introduction, he just needs a conclusion.

Our emcee must be a gentleman. The room from which he emerged proclaimed him so.

I could have listened to that introduction all evening, and for a while I thought I would have to.

☆ ☆ ☆

Who needs talent with courage like that?

I have traded many a poor speech for a good meal.

☆ ☆ ☆

The title of my speech is THE WORLD AND OTHER THINGS.

☆ ☆ ☆

A gingerale speaker is one that goes flat after being uncorked for a few moments.

☆ ☆ ☆

Thank you for the applause. It was scattered but sincere.

☆ ☆ ☆

Blessed are they who expect nothing for they shall not be disappointed.

☆ ☆ ☆

There are two things about the speaker that I would like to tell you. First, he has never been in jail, and second, I don't know why.

☆ ☆ ☆

Free speech isn't dead in Russia—only free speakers.

☆ ☆ ☆

This looks like a father-daughter banquet.

☆ ☆ ☆

I trace my ancestry all the way back to the Boston Tea Party to my great, great Aunt Ella —she was the last bag that they threw into the ocean.

☆ ☆ ☆

I was asked if I gave the same speech wherever I go.
I said, "Yes."
"Doesn't this present a problem when you are invited back?" asked one of my friends.
"No," I replied, "I've never been asked back."

☆ ☆ ☆

The obstetrician told the expectant mother, "I hope that you have a better delivery than your husband."

☆ ☆ ☆

SPORTS

A Little League baseball game was underway when a late-arriving spectator inquired as to the score.

"Twenty to nothing," replied a Little Leaguer.

"They're beating you bad," said the spectator.

"No, not really, we haven't been up to bat yet."

☆　☆　☆

A football team is eleven men and a bookie.

☆　☆　☆

A winner must first know what losing's like.
　　　　　　　　　　　　　　　—M. S. Forbes

☆　☆　☆

Three umpires were talking about the way they umpired the game. One fellow said they may be strikes or they may be balls but, anyway, he called them as he saw them. The second umpire said that be they strikes or be they balls he calls them exactly as they are. The third umpire said that so far as he was concerned they are neither strikes nor balls until he says what they are.

☆　☆　☆

I always umpired because I couldn't see well enough to bat.

☆　☆　☆

Babe Ruth said, "Stopping at third base adds no more to the score than striking out."

☆ ☆ ☆

A young lad said that baseball reminds him of his family, with mother pitching, dad catching, everyone taking a turn at bat, and the kids doing most of the fielding.

☆ ☆ ☆

In the David and Goliath story, we learn that Goliath probably had pituitary gland troubles. He stood nine feet, nine inches tall. He was a good-sized athlete and could have played on any team. But when David met him, he Bob Fellered a fast one and hit the giant right between the eyes. And the giant probably said, "I've never had anything like that enter my head before."

☆ ☆ ☆

When the going gets tough, the tough get going.

☆ ☆ ☆

A coach because of the very poor win-loss record was forced out of his position. Before relinquishing his office, he decided to leave two envelopes to his successor, and attached a note, "If things start going tough, you open the first envelope."

The successor was having a very bad season. He decided to open the first envelope, and it simply read, "Blame your predecessor."

As the season progressed, there was no improvement, so he decided to open the second envelope. In it was this note: "Make out two envelopes."

☆ ☆ ☆

The trouble with being a good sport is that you have to lose to prove it.

A spectator watching a football game on television called in inquiring as to the reason for one certain penalty. The sports announcer on the other end stated the penalty was for putting the ball in motion during a commercial.

☆   ☆   ☆

STOCK MARKET

When a friend asked Bernard Baruch whether the stock market would go up or down, he simply replied, "Undoubtedly."

The bulls get a little, the bears get a little, but the hogs get nothing.

Did you hear about the investor who is taking a course in veterinary medicine so that he will be able to look after the cats and dogs he bought in the recent bull market?

☆ ☆ ☆

During a recent bear market, a bar was featuring a new drink called "Stocks on the Rocks."

The market gyrates and I don't care
For I'm neither bull nor bear.
I make no foolish fiscal bets,
All my money's tied up in debts.

☆ ☆ ☆

"What do you think of getting measles at 71?"
"You think you got problems? I got Penn Central at 72."

☆ ☆ ☆

You never lose when you take a profit.

☆ ☆ ☆

A Canadian called his American friend and said that he had a hundred shares in a uranium mine and that he would sell them for a dollar a share. The American bought. A few days later the Canadian called and said, "That stock I sold you is up to $5 a share now, and I can let you have another 500 shares." The American bought.

A little later the Canadian called again and said, "You know, I've got some good news for you. That uranium stock that you have? The shares have now gone up to $10 a share and I can still let you have another thousand shares."

"In that case," replied the American, "I will sell."

After a long pause, the Canadian on the other end of the line remarked, "WHO TO?"

STREAKING

Streaking is an epidemic of the epidermis.

☆ ☆ ☆

A beautiful girl was streaking through the lobby of a plush hotel and was being pursued by an Army officer who was, to put it bluntly, nude.

At the court martial, the lawyer won an acquittal by virtue of the following paragraph in the Army Code of Law Manual: "It is not compulsory for an officer to wear a uniform at all times, as long as he is suitably garbed for the sport in which he is engaged."

☆ ☆ ☆

And then there was the father who worried because his young daughter recognized the streakers who were clad only in face masks.

☆ ☆ ☆

SUCCESS

It's thinking about the load that makes one tired.

☆ ☆ ☆

The turtle never makes progress until he sticks his neck out.

☆ ☆ ☆

The three most difficult things to do are to kiss your wife when she's leaning away from you; cross a fence when it's leaning toward you; and to alibi for something that you did wrong.

☆ ☆ ☆

Men do not stumble over mountains, only molehills.

☆ ☆ ☆

People can be divided into three groups— those who make things happen, those who watch things happen, and those who wonder what happened.

☆ ☆ ☆

Nothing is impossible for the man who doesn't have to do it himself.

☆ ☆ ☆

Dr. Arnold Lowe's formula: Do more than you need to do, learn more than you need to know, and be all that you can be.

☆ ☆ ☆

Successful man—one who makes more money than his wife can spend.

Successful woman—a woman who finds such a man.

☆ ☆ ☆

If at first you do succeed, try to hide your astonishment.

☆ ☆ ☆

Henry Ford said, "Coming together is a beginning; keeping together is progress; working together is success."

☆ ☆ ☆

How on earth were the Israelis so successful in winning the six-day war? They had to be, they were renting their equipment from Hertz.

☆ ☆ ☆

If at first you don't succeed, try again. And then if you don't succeed, give up. Why make a darned fool out of yourself.

☆ ☆ ☆

Henry Ford also said, "The harder I work, the luckier I get."

☆ ☆ ☆

To see the horizon one must look up.

☆ ☆ ☆

A formula for success—think of a product that costs a dime, sells for a dollar, and is habit-forming.

☆ ☆ ☆

Success comes by doing successfully one thing at a time.

☆ ☆ ☆

Behind every man
Who's achieved success
Stands a good wife
And the IRS.

☆ ☆ ☆

A successful journey is one with a destination.

☆ ☆ ☆

TAXES

"You have a nice home," said a stranger to the landowner. "I imagine it will be worth about $20,000."

"Oh, no, " replied the owner, "it's worth at least $50,000. Are you thinking about buying the home?"

"No," said the stranger, "I'm your local tax assessor."

The reason people have so many accountants doing their returns is that it saves them time— sometimes up to 20 years.

"I'm not in love with the present
For the good old days I pine
When the government lived within its income
And without so much of mine."

You can criticize the president
You can criticize the vice president
You can criticize the Congress
But you have to hand it to the IRS.

Despite the deterioration which may have occurred over the years, I've just discovered that husbands cannot claim depreciation on their wives or vice versa.

☆ ☆ ☆

Our peak earning years coincide with IRS's peak taking years.

☆   ☆   ☆

Income tax time is when you feel bled, white and blue.

☆   ☆   ☆

You've got to hand it to the tax people. If you don't, they'll come and get it.

☆   ☆   ☆

If you don't know the price of success, the IRS will gladly furnish you a tax table.

☆   ☆   ☆

Behind every man that has achieved success,
Stands a good woman and the IRS.

☆   ☆   ☆

A tax, a tax, another tax
What we need is tax insurance
To guard us on the day we drop
From over-taxed endurance.

—Anon

☆   ☆   ☆

TELEPHONE

The bathtub was invented in 1850, and the telephone in 1875. You could have sat in the tub for 25 years without being interrupted by a ringing telephone.

☆ ☆ ☆

The telephone rang at 3 a.m. "Are you awake?" inquired the caller.

"Yeah, I had to get up to answer the phone anyway."

☆ ☆ ☆

At 2 a.m. a man called his neighbor and asked him to quiet his barking dog. The next night at 3 a.m. the neighbor returned the call stating that he had no dog.

☆ ☆ ☆

TEXAS

A man in New Jersey discovered a use for frogskins, so he advertised in the Wall Street Journal. A gentleman from Texas replied to the ad and stated that he could supply all the frogskins desired. The man from New Jersey put in an order for two dozen frogskins. He waited and waited for the supply to arrive. Finally a small package arrived in the mail. When he opened it up there was one lone frogskin with a note attached to it. "The noise fooled me."

A Texan visiting Australia was telling that it took big saws to cut some of their homegrown watermelons. As they were visiting, a kangaroo bounced by, and the Texan inquired of the Australian what the animal was. The Australian said, "That's not an animal, that's a grasshopper."

Everything is big in Texas including their dust storms. One day while driving in Texas a visitor noticed a cowboy hat in the ditch. He ran down and scraped the sand off the hat, got past the brim, kept going and pretty soon discovered the hat was being worn by someone who had become totally imbedded in the sand. As he got below the eyebrows, below the nose, and below the mouth, the man said, "Go back to the car and get a shovel. I'm on horseback."

☆ ☆ ☆

Here is to Texas and all other out-lying states.

Then there was the Texan that couldn't decide whether Texas has the world's largest or smallest midgets.

If all the ice glaciers in Alaska should melt, Texas would become one of our smallest states.

TRAVEL AND TOURISM

Florida has two main industries, tourists and alligators, and they skin them both.

Folks from the north going south for the winter spend a lot of time getting a suntan, but when they get their bills, they turn white.

No one should ever ask where a person is from. If he is from South Dakota, he will tell you. If not, it will embarrass him.

The most lonesome feeling I ever had was going the wrong way on a one-way street. The cop stopped me and asked me where I was going. I told him wherever it was I must be late because everyone else was already coming back.

Travel broadens one—so does sitting at home in an easy chair.

Short visits make for long friends.

Men state that most vacations are disguised shopping trips.

A gentleman was sitting in a bar reading an advertisement in the local Want Ad section which read, "Would like to have person to accompany me on trip to Florida."

After several drinks, he left the bar and drove up to the address given in the ad. He knocked on the door. The man came to the door and asked what the caller wanted.

"I came in response to your ad. I just wanted to tell you that I can't go."

UNDERTAKER

An undertaker is the type of person that will let you down in the end.

Down South they call an undertaker a Southern planter.

It isn't the cough that sends you off,
It's the coffin that they send you off in.

An undertaker's business is always going into the hole.

Undertaking is primarily an ushering out profession.

WAITER

"I don't like all these flies that are flying around here."

"Well, just point out the ones you do like, sir, and I'll swat the rest."

WEATHER

In our section of the country we always get two rains—one too early and one too late.

"Do you get a lot of snow in your section of the country?"
"No, but a lot of it goes through here."

We have no weather to report this morning, the temperature is zero.

This unusual weather is more unusual than usual.

☆ ☆ ☆

It was so cold the other morning that when I set out a pan of boiling water it froze so fast that the ice was still warm.

It's been so dry lately that the rain that we did get had only 40% moisture.

He holds so many degrees that his friends call him Mr. Fahrenheit.

☆ ☆ ☆

It was so dry that trees chased dogs.

☆ ☆ ☆

Our drouth was so bad, that during the time of Noah's flood, we got only 2½ inches of rain in our section of the country.

The drouth was so bad, and our hogs so thin, that when we sent them to the slaughterhouse they were able to make bacon that had rinds on both sides.

An old timer was reminiscing about the severe drought of the 30's. "Why, even the earth got big cracks in it. One noon I accidentally dropped a wrench into a crack on my way to lunch, and when I got back, I could still hear it dropping."

What's so wonderful about living where it gets to 30 degrees below zero in the wintertime? Well, the big attraction is that there are no mosquitoes.

My farm is located too far north for the south rains, and too far south for the north rains.

WHO RULES

I rule the roost, but my wife rules the rooster.

A lion was walking through the forest taking a poll to determine who was the greatest among all the wildlife animals. When he saw the hippopotamus, he inquired, "Who is king of the forest?"

"You are," said the hippopotamus.

Next he met a giraffe. "Who is the king of the forest?" he inquired.

"You are," said the giraffe.

Next he met the elephant. He gave him a good rap on the knee and said, "And who is king of the forest?"

The elephant picked him up in his trunk, and swung him against the tree. As the lion slid down, brushing himself off, he said, "You don't have to get so mad just because you don't know the right answer."

☆　☆　☆

WOMEN

Women have always had the last word, and now they add lib.

☆ ☆ ☆

Women started the liberation movement because they were tired of dancing backwards. And now when they go to the filling station, they say, "Fill him up."

☆ ☆ ☆

In Russia, Good Humor men are ladies.

☆ ☆ ☆

Women have always been a side issue.

☆ ☆ ☆

A thing of beauty is a job forever.

☆ ☆ ☆

Women are remarkable creatures whereas men can't say much.

☆ ☆ ☆

She sends me out with my conscience while she sits at home flirting with her imagination.

☆ ☆ ☆

I guess my wife quit smoking cigarets. I found cigar butts in the ashtray.

☆ ☆ ☆

My wife went through three red lights the other day—two of them were on the back of a truck.

When a woman sticks her hand out of a car window it means that the window is down.

If a woman is a member of the opposite sex, what am I?

When man was first introduced to woman, Adam went up to Eve and said, "Madam, I'm Adam."

Eve asked Adam, "Do you still love me?" And Adam replied, "Who else?"

The Russians have discovered something that will do the work of ten men—namely, ten women.

You can always surprise your husband on your anniversary just by mentioning it.

WORK

God made the world, but the Dutch made Holland.

The only thing worse than work is looking for work.

Henry Ford was a lucky man. The harder he worked, the luckier he got.

It is better to put 10 men to work than to do the work of ten men.

Work is one of God's greatest gifts.

Work ethic: Once our people were busy as beavers, now they are as playful as otters.

"I'm puzzled," said the doctor, "you seem to be suffering from overwork, but nobody does that any more."

YOUTH

I'm for it.

I never censure or berate my children
When they've incensed me.
I'm fearful lest they'll demonstrate
Against me.

Barefoot boy with cheek of tan,
Are you a boy, my little man?
Or are you, with your hair aswirl,
No boy at all? Are you a girl?
And in those faded jeans with patches
And shirt so tattered (nothing matches),
Are you a starveling, lacking care?
Or offspring of a millionaire?

—Richard Armour

171

UNCLASSIFIED

"No, Lulu, an alabaster isn't an illegitimate Mohammedan."

☆　☆　☆

This is my first visit to your blighted area.

☆　☆　☆

May I present my wife?
No, thanks, I already have one.

☆　☆　☆

Fanny Foxe—
She was only a stripper
At the Silver Slipper,
But she had her ways and means.

☆　☆　☆

Said one strawberry to another, if I had not been planted in the same bed with you, we wouldn't be in this jam together.

☆　☆　☆

Well-reared girls shouldn't wear slacks.

☆　☆　☆

The bunny girls at the Playboy Clubs are on strike. They want more lettuce.

☆　☆　☆

Are you troubled by improper thoughts?
No, I get a kick out of them.

☆　☆　☆

Halitosis is better than no breath at all.

Her breath takes her beauty away.

I never met a man I didn't like. I forget now whether it was Will Rogers or Elizabeth Taylor that said that.

I'm real good to my wife, I never go home.

Wherever you go, there you are.

All the men in Washington are on their toes —seems that the President has raised all the urinals in the Capitol 12 inches.

The statue of Stalin in Lenin Square is so big that it gives shade from the sun in the summer, protection from the wind in the winter, and gives birds an opportunity to speak for all.

The father told his son, "I can see right through that girl's intrigue."
"Yes," replied the son, "but that's the way they all dress nowadays."

☆　☆　☆

Did you hear what happened to the girl with the cotton stockings?
Nothing.

☆　☆　☆

Three out of every four people have a mental problem. If the three people that you're with look normal, then you're the one with the problem.

Nonchalance: The ability to look like an owl when you've behaved like an ass.

"Bobby, where is the English Channel?"
"I don't know, teacher, we can't get it on our TV."

As more and more women become successes in fields once dominated by men, one wonders: Is it because women don't have wives to support?

Why is it that there is never enough time to do a job right, but there always seems to be enough time to do it over?

Don't put off until tomorrow what you can do today. If you enjoy it, you can do it again tomorrow—if you're young enough.

I was kidding one of my good friends the other day, and he told me, "Al, you can go straight to hell."
I quickly replied, "George, that's the first time I've ever had an invitation to your home."

☆   ☆   ☆

Here's to Adam,
Father of us all,
He was Johnny on the spot,
When the leaves began to fall.

No more talk about giving South Dakota back to our Native Americans—they've suffered enough already.

Why am I here? Last night I had a dream. I dreamed I died and went to heaven. When I arrived at the Pearly Gates, St. Peter said, "There is no room for you here. But I can tell you where to go."

When I got to that other place—a very hot one—a fellow that called himself the devil said, "We have no room for you here."

And that's why I'm here tonight.

If a cluttered desk is indicative of a cluttered mind, is an empty desk indicative of an empty mind?

I think my husband would make a good member of the Ku Klux Klan—he's such a devil under the sheet.

A girl's plans for the future seldom take shape before she does.

☆   ☆   ☆

Boss: I have good news for all of the employees today. We have complied with all federal, state and local regulations. All forms have been completed and sent in. I also have some bad news—the company is filing for bankruptcy.

He: I'd kiss you, but I have scruples.
She: Oh, that's o.k. I've been vaccinated for that.

Many a woman has started out playing with fire and ended up cooking over it.

I was born a Lutheran and raised a Lutheran. I'll always be a Lutheran. No one is going to make a Christian out of me!

A gossip is a person with a keen sense of rumor.

I don't know how old he is, but I would judge that he is somewhere between sin and Sun City.

The habits of rabbits
Are such it's agreed
That dozens of cousins
Are common indeed.

☆ ☆ ☆

A race horse is an animal that can take hundreds of people for a ride at the same time.

A new hotel in Las Vegas caters exclusively to about-to-be-divorcees. It's called the Jiltin-Hilton.

Smile—it adds to your face value.

Keep smiling. It makes people wonder what you've been up to.

ABOUT THE AUTHOR

Al Schock is an achiever. It will come as no surprise to his many friends that he's now writing books. Having spoken at or emceed more than 2,000 functions, he has written a much-needed book on EMCEEING (AND UNRELATED ITEMS) based on his own experiences. Al believes that too many of our meetings, conventions, and banquets are poorly planned, humdrum, non-productive, and just plain boring.

This compilation of anecdotes, stories, one-liners, and good advice is typical of Al. It represents an enlargement of one of the chapters in his book. If Al has something good going for him, he wants to share it with his fellow man. As a matter of fact, he insists on it.

A veteran of World War II, holder of the Bronze Star and Purple Heart, he came out of army hospitals to get a master's degree at the University of Wisconsin. After a two-year stint as a professor at South Dakota State University, he and his brother Ozzie started a dairy operation with $500 of operating capital and a pile of bank loan rejection slips. The dairy and related businesses that the Schock brothers founded are now doing sales in excess of $30 million annually. Al has a world-wide reputation for developing new processes for the manufacture of a superior cottage cheese and other specialty dairy products.

A national, state and community leader, who has traveled world-wide, he has

—promoted industrial development and diversification in his agricultural home state;

—served as chairman of the Board of Governors of Lions International;

—been a candidate for the United States Senate;

—participated in a trade mission to the Mideast in 1975;

—been elected a director of the National Water Resources Association;

—aided the visually handicapped;

—been president of the Chamber of Commerce;

—headed the United Fund;

—been and is a member of the Board of Regents of Augustana College;

—spearheaded many, many other projects with special concern for the young and the old.

A gentle man with a keen wit and a lively sense of humor, Al enjoys a good story. This anthology of some of his favorites, in addition to being enjoyable reading, will provide emcees and speakers a ready source of usable material to enliven their presentations.

MELVIN POWERS SELF-IMPROVEMENT LIBRARY

CHESS & CHECKERS

_____ BEGINNER'S GUIDE TO WINNING CHESS Fred Reinfeld	5.00
_____ CHESS IN TEN EASY LESSONS Larry Evans	5.00
_____ CHESS MADE EASY Milton L. Hanauer	3.00
_____ CHESS PROBLEMS FOR BEGINNERS edited by Fred Reinfeld	2.00
_____ CHESS SECRETS REVEALED Fred Reinfeld	2.00
_____ CHESS TACTICS FOR BEGINNERS edited by Fred Reinfeld	4.00
_____ CHESS THEORY & PRACTICE Morry & Mitchell	2.00
_____ HOW TO WIN AT CHECKERS Fred Reinfeld	3.00
_____ 1001 BRILLIANT WAYS TO CHECKMATE Fred Reinfeld	4.00
_____ 1001 WINNING CHESS SACRIFICES & COMBINATIONS Fred Reinfeld	4.00
_____ SOVIET CHESS Edited by R. G. Wade	3.00

HOBBIES

_____ BEACHCOMBING FOR BEGINNERS Norman Hickin	2.00
_____ BLACKSTONE'S MODERN CARD TRICKS Harry Blackstone	3.00
_____ BLACKSTONE'S SECRETS OF MAGIC Harry Blackstone	3.00
_____ COIN COLLECTING FOR BEGINNERS Burton Hobson & Fred Reinfeld	3.00
_____ ENTERTAINING WITH ESP Tony 'Doc' Shiels	2.00
_____ 400 FASCINATING MAGIC TRICKS YOU CAN DO Howard Thurston	4.00
_____ HOW I TURN JUNK INTO FUN AND PROFIT Sari	3.00
_____ HOW TO WRITE A HIT SONG & SELL IT Tommy Boyce	7.00
_____ JUGGLING MADE EASY Rudolf Dittrich	3.00
_____ MAGIC FOR ALL AGES Walter Gibson	4.00
_____ MAGIC MADE EASY Byron Wels	2.00
_____ STAMP COLLECTING FOR BEGINNERS Burton Hobson	3.00

HUMOR

_____ HOW TO BE A COMEDIAN FOR FUN & PROFIT King & Laufer	2.00
_____ HOW TO FLATTEN YOUR TUSH Coach Marge Reardon	2.00
_____ HOW TO MAKE LOVE TO YOURSELF Ron Stevens & Joy Grdnic	3.00
_____ JOKE TELLER'S HANDBOOK Bob Orben	4.00
_____ JOKES FOR ALL OCCASIONS Al Schock	4.00
_____ 2000 NEW LAUGHS FOR SPEAKERS Bob Orben	4.00
_____ 2,500 JOKES TO START 'EM LAUGHING Bob Orben	5.00

SPORTS

_____ BICYCLING FOR FUN AND GOOD HEALTH Kenneth E. Luther	2.00
_____ BILLIARDS—Pocket • Carom • Three Cushion Clive Cottingham, Jr.	3.00
_____ CAMPING-OUT 101 Ideas & Activities Bruno Knobel	2.00
_____ COMPLETE GUIDE TO FISHING Vlad Evanoff	2.00
_____ HOW TO IMPROVE YOUR RACQUETBALL Lubarsky Kaufman & Scagnetti	3.00
_____ HOW TO WIN AT POCKET BILLIARDS Edward D. Knuchell	5.00
_____ JOY OF WALKING Jack Scagnetti	3.00
_____ LEARNING & TEACHING SOCCER SKILLS Eric Worthington	3.00
_____ MOTORCYCLING FOR BEGINNERS I. G. Edmonds	3.00
_____ RACQUETBALL FOR WOMEN Toni Hudson, Jack Scagnetti & Vince Rondone	3.00
_____ RACQUETBALL MADE EASY Steve Lubarsky, Rod Delson & Jack Scagnetti	4.00
_____ SECRET OF BOWLING STRIKES Dawson Taylor	3.00
_____ SECRET OF PERFECT PUTTING Horton Smith & Dawson Taylor	3.00
_____ SOCCER—The Game & How to Play It Gary Rosenthal	3.00
_____ STARTING SOCCER Edward F. Dolan, Jr.	3.00

TENNIS LOVERS' LIBRARY

_____ BEGINNER'S GUIDE TO WINNING TENNIS Helen Hull Jacobs	2.00
_____ HOW TO BEAT BETTER TENNIS PLAYERS Loring Fiske	4.00
_____ HOW TO IMPROVE YOUR TENNIS—Style, Strategy & Analysis C. Wilson	2.00
_____ INSIDE TENNIS—Techniques of Winning Jim Leighton	3.00
_____ PLAY TENNIS WITH ROSEWALL Ken Rosewall	2.00
_____ PSYCH YOURSELF TO BETTER TENNIS Dr. Walter A. Luszki	2.00
_____ TENNIS FOR BEGINNERS, Dr. H. A. Murray	2.00
_____ TENNIS MADE EASY Joel Brecheen	3.00
_____ WEEKEND TENNIS—How to Have Fun & Win at the Same Time Bill Talbert	3.00
_____ WINNING WITH PERCENTAGE TENNIS—Smart Strategy Jack Lowe	2.00

The books listed above can be obtained from your book dealer or directly from
Melvin Powers. When ordering, please remit 50¢ per book postage & handling.
Send for our free illustrated catalog of self-improvement books.

Melvin Powers
12015 Sherman Road, No. Hollywood, California 91605